To Cynthia
with best ~

27 June 1987

A World of Love

an anthology compiled by
GODFREY SMITH
from nominations made by
readers of the *Sunday Times*

ELM TREE BOOKS

London

For Picco again

First published in Great Britain 1982
by Elm Tree Books/Hamish Hamilton Ltd
Garden House 57-59 Long Acre London WC2E 9JZ

Compilation, introduction and commentary copyright © 1982
by Godfrey Smith
See further copyright acknowledgements on page 120

British Library Cataloguing in Publication Data

A World of love.
    1. Love-Literary collections
    I. Smith, Godfrey
    808.8'0354   PN6071.L7

ISBN 0-241-10714-8

Typeset by Saildean Ltd
Printed and bound in Great Britain by
Richard Clay (The Chaucer Press) Ltd, Bungay, Suffolk

Contents

Introduction

This book came about by accident, as things should in the world of love. Jilly Cooper had sent me a paperback copy of her enchanting anthology *The British In Love* and I noted in my *Sunday Times* column that, while it contained many trusted favourites, it couldn't include everything one would have liked, since no two people have precisely the same tastes. So why didn't readers help me compile an anthology of our own?

There was to be no boundary in time or language. Prose and poetry would be equally welcome. Nor would we confine ourselves to the written word: quotes from film, television or radio would count as well. There would be some bubbly for the best.

The letters cascaded in. Their range was astonishing. There were quotations not merely, as one might have expected, from French, Spanish, Italian and German authors, but also from China, Japan, India, and Burma. We had Latin and Greek, but we also had Groucho Marx and Dorothy Parker. We had an inscription from an Egyptian papyrus, and a quote from *The Times* personal column last Valentine's day. We had a line from an old Bogart movie, and a translation from the Sanskrit. The mailbag was enormous, and would have defeated me without Jilly's help. As it was, we had a long but pleasurable slog to find the winners.

What were we to do with the rest? The only answer seemed to be a book, and that is just what Elm Tree suggested. Here it is.

1

My own role is an odd one, since although I suggested the party I did not invite the guests, and could only stand at the door as, in American parlance, a combined greeter and bouncer. This is no way to duck the responsibility for the result; only to disclaim credit for the depth of reference evinced. What we have here is simply an assortment of statements about love made over the centuries by people of diverse backgrounds, as they were recalled by the collective memory of my readers in the early spring of 1981.

I could give them a mild bollocking (and did) for omitting Spender's high-octane *O night, O trembling night* and grumble that I could have done with more MacNeice, particularly that stretch about the girl whose mind was like the wind on a sea of wheat. I was astonished that no one had offered Meredith's *Love in the Valley,* surely, though uneven and over-long, one of the greatest love poems in the language. There was no Eliot either, not surprisingly perhaps since he is not essentially a love poet, despite the grave beauty of *A Dedication to my Wife.*

Still, it seemed to me that the treasure trove we did discover was rich enough and rare enough to outweigh such lacunae. Contrariwise, my correspondents occasionally weighed in with a very familiar quotation which I've included not only because some reader will be coming across it for the first time, but also because so much jam cries out for a slice or two of bread.

The real pleasure of a column like mine is not that the readers write it for you (as some curmudgeons have suggested) but that a dialogue develops between us from which everybody learns to enjoy something new.

I still remember coming as a schoolboy on a piece by Peter Quennell which enthused over the sophisticated brilliance of Aldous Huxley's novels. That opened a door for me which led into an unexpected pavilion of new pleasure. I like to believe that something like that might happen to one or two people who read *A World of Love.*

Cyril Connolly tells a story about the American aesthete and literary miniaturist Logan Pearsall Smith who, a few days before his death, was asked if he had found any meaning in life. 'Yes,' he replied. 'There is a meaning, at least, for me, there is one thing that matters – to set a chime of words tinkling in the minds of a few fastidious people.'

'And the State, Logan,' the friend went on, 'the Family, the International Situation, Russia, India?' Propped up on his pillows he waved all this away with his hand. 'A chime of words,' he repeated, 'a few discriminating people.'

I have tried to take the reader through *A World of Love* with a linking commentary, but before we start our journey, a few preliminary thoughts on the nature of love seem worth saying.

The first and most obvious point is to marvel at the staying power of the mighty impulse. With the position of women in society changing so rapidly, it would have been tempting to postulate that the role of romantic love would be changing fast too. A brief formulation of this kind of theory would go as follows.

Women, trapped by their biological imperatives and systematically deprived of their political and economic rights over the centuries, have been bamboozled into accepting the emotional solace of romantic love instead. From the rise of the troubadors, they have been put on a pedestal: a very good position, as one cynic observed, for looking up their skirts. Come to think of it, there is not much room for anything on a pedestal: travel, adventure, change, experiment. Men were deceivers ever, and swear their eternal allegiance in many an oath – and ne'er a true one, as Jessica commented. This extravagant courtship had to be validated by a legal and binding contract of marriage to guarantee woman that she had got, and would keep, a breadwinner for her house and a father for her children.

The confidence trick was cemented into an *idée recue* by the rise of the consumer society, the apotheosis of domesticity, and the proliferation of the sexist media.

This travesty of natural justice, the theory would run on, lasted a millenium, and has been overtaken by the invention of the Pill, the coming of equal pay, and the rise of Women's Lib. The transient partner, the lesbian alternative, the commune and the crèche, the access to easy divorce and the unending quest for orgasm are replacing the old verities.

In such a brave new world, the old romantic clichés are overthrown. Reality has triumphed over myth, truth over fiction. Where sentimentality once ruled, sensuality now holds sway. What has been lost to romance has been gained by reason.

There is a scintilla of truth in all this. Ancient wrongs have been righted. Women do have more say in their own destinies and more control over the management of their own bodies. Men do now quite naturally reverse roles, change nappies and attend accouchements. Whether this makes people happier is a nice point. What is beyond question is that they now have infinitely more scope to choose the nature of their happiness or unhappiness.

What, though, in all this storm and flux, has happened to the notion of love? What, if anything, can we see through the massive fall-out after the mighty bang that ended the old order?

First, I suggest, a profound change in the relation between class and sex. Romance began as a courtly skill and the prerogative of the upper class who were the only ones with the leisure to enjoy its intricacies and nuances. Few Victorian novels got far without depicting an upper-class love affair, and this convention may be said to have continued until the middle of this century in the polished entertainment provided by Evelyn Waugh and Nancy Mitford – politically deplorable though they no doubt were.

I find it hard to see how an ambitious young novelist starting work today could pull off a serious aristocratic love story. The aristo in love has become a figure of fun, skulking in the bushes at Blandings Castle or at best waiting in the wings of a William Douglas-Home play.

Yet the yearning for romance flourishes and is nourished by the booming house of Mills and Boon. Miss Barbara Cartland has become a millionaire simply because women want to go on being bamboozled. Only in pages like hers can heroines still swoon into aristocratic arms (unless we include the historical novel, a sub-division of the genre). They know perfectly well that it's rubbish, but it is such harmless and diverting rubbish. The same force may be seen in the near-universal enthusiasm for the Royal Wedding, which was enjoyed at different levels of sophistication. It could be relished even by those who saw in it no more than a new and spectacular addition to the theatre of the absurd.

Even the middle-class love affair, which has held the centre of our imaginative stage so brilliantly and so long, is beginning to look and sound perilously close to self-parody. *Brief Encounter,* taken *au pied de la lettre* only a generation ago, is now seen by the young as incredible at best and ludicrous at all times. The middle-class lovers in the novels of Iris Murdoch and Fay Weldon are anti-heroes and para-heroines; impotent fumblers and neurotic bitches. They are not to be taken seriously. The goddess has bestowed her favours elsewhere.

A new voice has been heard in the land, strident yet compelling: the voice of the worker as lover. Where before he had been a comic bit-player, he was now cast in the lead. Novelists like David Storey in *This Sporting Life* introduced us to the inarticulate but chaotically male animal whose sexuality is expressed in body language and whose passion is demonstrated by a belt round the lug-hole.

It appeared in 1960, the same year that *Lady Chatterley's Lover,* pioneer of the genre, at last found legal acceptance in Britain after an epic legal case. At the Royal Court, John Osborne had already introduced us to one of the most compulsive lovers of our time: Jimmy Porter, sweet-stall vendor and *sansculotte,* owner of a gritty eloquence born out of pain and a talent for breathtaking abuse, all encased in an innate vulnerability that caused women on stage and off to fall at his feet.

Jimmy and Alison play at being squirrels and bears, and in his final speech Osborne makes Jimmy work the little furry animals into a complex metaphor of modern love. It was a speech which engendered writhing embarrassment in the old style of playgoer nourished on the pabulum of Binkie Beaumont, but at once struck a chord in the hearts and minds of a rising generation of formally qualified but still socially disoriented young people.

Probably lovers have given each other soppy names since the beginning; they had not been made so wincingly public before. The dam broke, and now each Valentine's Day the once chaste columns of *The Times* are crammed with thousands of loving messages ostensibly exchanged between small furry animals with bright eyes and bushy tails. (We include a typical one in this anthology.) By the same token, the old bedecked and beribboned Valentine has given way to the flip card with an ostensibly straight-faced endearment at the front and a disparaging (and often rude) *double entendre* inside.

If a personal instance of this new, cool style may be forgiven, one of my daughters, in Oxford for her entrance examination, left a loving message for a boy-friend due to take a similar hurdle at another college a few days later. It read, in its entirety: 'Sock it to them, shitface.' I suppose what this kind of signal really means is: I love you and wish you well, but am not going to be such a fool as to say so literally. It is that distrust of the committal to love so neatly caught by Dorothy Parker: By the time you swear you're his/Shivering and sighing/And he swears his passion is/Infinite, undying – /Lady, make a note of this:/One of you is lying.

Thus the style and form in which the language of love is expressed alters dramatically: whether the nature of the emotion or quality of the relationship has fundamentally changed seems open to doubt. Marriage as an institution continues to boom, and though divorce releases an increasing number from over-hasty misalliance, the prevalence of second, third, or even fourth marriages underlines the popularity of the notoriously complex and hazardous institution. There are men – and women – who choose to face life alone: but they are not many.

Whether the modes of modern love will continue to be delineated by the written word is questionable. The tally of formally educated literates continues its upward swing on the graph; but so does the sales curve of audio-visual hardware. The pop lyric, like the pop melody, all too often excruciatingly banal, very occasionally rises to astonishing levels of articulation and even beauty: witness the work of Lennon and McCartney, Simon and Garfunkel. 'The winds of March that made my heart a dancer' is not unworthy of Auden himself on a so-so day, though in fact from *These Foolish Things;* and it is reassuring to know that Auden enjoyed reciting the lyrics of shows like *Guys and Dolls.*

The rise of the pop lyric could speed the isolation of the literary writer in a small, isolated enclave, unable to communicate with anything but a tiny cult audience. I hope not. It is no doubt yet another function of the celebrated generation gap that I find memorable lines of poetry stop being written (for me, that is) around 1950. I admire the technical excellence of Geoffrey Hill and Seamus Heaney, but their work simply refuses to echo in my head.

Conceivably the external world in which the poetry of Eliot and Auden, MacNeice and Spender was made proved a fiercer crucible; perhaps all experience was heightened by wars and rumours of wars: I don't know. All I know is that nothing written in the last thirty years moves me anywhere near as much as MacNeice's *Time Was Away* or Auden's *Lay Your Sleeping Head, My Love* (both of which, incidentally, find a place in this anthology while Hill and Heaney do not).

It is time we were on our way: first, though, here are a few ground rules. The memories of readers are usually found on checking to be unimpeachable, but not always, and we have tried to authenticate every quotation independently. That has not always proved possible.

Most authors of prose or poetry quoted are easily established; occasionally we have had to credit that prolific word-spinner Anon. Where we were wrong in this attribution we should be glad to be corrected. Most readers wrote in a clear (and often beautiful) hand; occasionally they have omitted their own names or addresses or sometimes both. Such gaps will be filled in any subsequent editions should they be furnished.

Where readers gave just a few lines from a work we have generally followed and given no more or less. We have used the translations offered and more than once, gratefully, a reader's own translation. We have also included one poem by a reader and one previously unpublished letter written by a reader's ancestor which was clearly worth its place. Some two thirds of contributions published were sent by women.

To sum up, what this little anthology tries to offer is not erudition but entertainment. It will not increase by one whit the sum total of human knowledge, but it might open a door for an occasional reader as Peter Quennell once opened a door for me; at any rate, I hope so.

What I think finally that these pages do reveal – and despite the surface show of violent change we have discussed – is the extraordinary durability and immutability of human love across centuries, cultures, creeds and continents. Probably only feats of human engineering still, thank heaven, at the test-tube stage will change that:

And I think with joy how whatever, now or in future, the system/Nothing whatever can take/The people away, there will always be people/For friends or for lovers though perhaps/The conditions of love will be changed and its vices diminished/And affection not lapse/To narrow possessiveness, jealousy founded on vanity.

So wrote my favourite Thirties poet MacNeice, soon after the bust-up of his first marriage, but with love to come and many more lines that would chime in the head still before him, as we shall now see.

The Quest of Love

I hesitated about starting with Bertrand Russell because the nitty gritty of his long romantic career is often totally at odds with the power and elegance in which he described it. Still, we must not argue ad hominem *and the apologia for love with which Russell prefaced his autobiography would be hard to beat for eloquence and precision.*

Love is the key with which we escape the prison of loneliness, and it is in that new-won liberty that our troubles begin. Never mind. Ecstasy, cries Russell, that was what it was all about; and how ruthlessly he pursued it! With what energy and ingenuity did this libidinous little leprechaun pursue each new love; with what crisp resolution did he throw over each old love!

Often ludicrous, as when a distressing infection of the gums halted his idyll with Lady Ottoline Morell, he still deserves some access to the nirvana he claims to have found at the end, if only on the basis of his single-minded obsession.

We follow with the caveat of another philosopher and prolific novelist with a tolerant and observant eye for the follies of the human heart. A form of insanity, adjudicates Iris Murdoch, and on the uncluttered evidence, she must be right.

No one puts the sexual rage more magnificently than Emily Brontë, and this passage from Wuthering Heights *was sent by more than one reader. Yes, it is insane, she says in effect; but don't try to stop me: I have absolutely no choice.*

Prologue to *Autobiography 1872-1914* by Bertrand Russell
contributed by Sandra Fox, Watford

I have sought love, first, because it brings ecstasy – ecstasy
so great that I would often have sacrificed all the rest of life
for a few hours of this joy. I have sought it, next, because it
relieves loneliness – that terrible loneliness in which one
shivering consciousness looks over the rim of the world into
the cold unfathomable lifeless abyss. I have sought it,
finally, because in the union of love I have seen, in a mystic
minature, the prefiguring vision of the heaven that saints
and poets have imagined. This is what I sought, and
though it might seem too good for human life, this is
what – at last – I have found.

Bradley Pearson's view of being in love, from *The Black
Prince* by Iris Murdoch
contributed by Diana Chapman, London

It is, as I remarked, a form of insanity. Is it not insane to
concentrate one's attention exclusively on one person, to
drain the rest of the world of meaning, to have no
thoughts, no feelings, no being except in relation to the
beloved? What the beloved 'is like' or 'is really like' matters
not a fig. Of course some people go crazy about people
whom other people think worthless. 'Why did she fall for
the leader of the band?' is an eternal question. We are
stunned when we see those whom we esteem enslaved by
the vulgar, the frivolous, or the base. But even if the man
or woman were so fine and so wise that their claim to be
such could be denied by no one, it would still be a form of
madness to direct upon him or upon her the kind of
exclusive worshipping attention in which being in love
consists.

From *Wuthering Heights* by Emily Brontë
contributed by Karen Berrill, Colchester

I cannot express it; but surely you and everybody have a notion that there is, or should be an existence of yours beyond you. What were the use of my creation if I were entirely contained here? My great miseries in this world have been Heathcliff's miseries, and I watched and felt each from the beginning; my great thought in living is himself. If all else perished, and *he* remained, I should continue to be; and if all else remained, and he were annihilated, the universe would turn to a mighty stranger. I should not seem part of it. My love for Linton is like the foliage in the woods. Time will change it, I'm well aware, as winter changes the trees. My love for Heathcliff resembles the eternal rocks beneath – a source of little delight, but necessary. Nelly, I *am* Heathcliff – he's always, always in my mind – not as a pleasure, any more than I am always a pleasure to myself – but as my own being – so, don't talk of our separation again – it is impracticable ... '

The idea of love so overwhelming that it is pointless to resist is echoed in Rosemary Hawley Jarman's We Speak No Treason *('a super book,' says Veronica Savage, 'and this paragraph I have always remembered in particular'); and again in Tennyson's* Guinevere, *perhaps one of the earliest and most lyrical formulations of the guilty refrain, 'We can't go on meeting like this.'*

From *We Speak No Treason* by Rosemary Hawley Jarman
contributed by Veronica Savage, Guildford

And had I been an old old woman with three husbands
buried and twice as many children, or had I been a
coal-black queen from the East with the whole of Byzan-
tium under my hand; or had I been an idiot with no
tongue, no ears, and only eyes, eyes to see whom I saw
then, and a heart to feel as my heart felt; had I been any of
these, I would have done as I did. And being what I was, a
virgin maid, with but an armoured dream to cherish, I
looked that night upon a man, and loved.

From *Idylls of the King* by Alfred, Lord Tennyson
contributed by Jenny Williamson, Croydon

> .... and at the last she said,
> 'O Lancelot, get thee hence to thine own land,
> For if thou tarry we shall meet again,
> And if we meet again, some evil chance
> Will make the smouldering scandal break and blaze
> Before the people, and our Lord the King.'
> And Lancelot ever promised, but remain'd,
> And still they met and met....

*The sense of love as an inevitable force which it is better not to resist
is taken up by Cervantes in* Don Quixote *in a passage very kindly
translated for us by reader Anna Kirwan. Don't be afraid; but we do
fear what we can't control, as Clemence Dane clearly sees, even
when it is transfiguring. Laurie Lee catches the narcissism of love
but accedes to its incandescent qualities: it makes the skin glow like
some insubstantial Vitamin E.*

Our anonymous Elizabethan sees it as a bagatelle. As Anne Zwack, who sent it, remarks, the Elizabethans had an ironic, uncloying, yet compelling way of putting it. The Jacobeans who succeeded them were no great sentimentalists either, as we clearly see from that spendid quatrain by Sir John Suckling, described by his contemporary D'Avenant as a sparkling wit, and the greatest gallant and gamester of his day. He invented the game of cribbage, and evidently did not believe that love or anything else should be cabin'd, cribb'd, or confin'd.

Finally in our opening statements about love, we have the cynical verdict of Conrad Aiken. Michael Croft, Director of the National Youth Theatre, wrote to say that he first came across it in the Salvation Army hostel in Reykjavik when trekking across Iceland in the summer vacation of 1948 with his actor friend and fellow undergraduate William Russell. 'The verse well suited my mood of the time,' Michael comments, 'following an unfulfilled Oxford affair. It now perfectly describes my feelings about the Arts Council.' It's a sour note to finish on, but have no fear, we shall be hearing from Aiken in quite a different mood later.

From *Don Quixote* by Miguel de Cervantes
contributed by Anna Kirwan, Wallasey, Merseyside

Love, I've heard it said, sometimes flies and sometimes walks, with one it runs and with another it creeps, some it cools and some it burns, some it wounds and others it kills, in one moment it starts its race of passion and in the same instant concludes and ends it; in the morning it makes seige to a fortress and by evening conquers it, for there is no force that can resist it. That being so, what is it that frightens you?

From *Will Shakespeare* by Clemence Dane
contributed by Mrs Betty Gearing, Richmond

> What is this love?
> What is this awful spirit and unknown
> That mates the suns and gives a bird his tune?
> What is this stirring at the roots of the world?
> What is this secret child that leaps in the womb
> Of life? What is this wind, whence does it blow,
> And why? And falls upon us like the flame
> Of Pentecost, haphazard. What is this dire
> And holy ghost that will not let us two
> For no prayers sake nor good deeds sake nor pain
> Nor pity, have peace, and live at ease and die
> As the leaves die?

From *I Can't Stay Long* by Laurie Lee

To be in love.... is to take on the pent-house of living, that topmost toppling tower, perpetually lit by the privileged radiance of well-being which sets one apart from the nether world. Born, we are mortal, dehydrated, ordinary; love is the oil that plumps one up, dilates the eyes, puts a glow on the skin, lifts us free from the weight of time, and helps us see in some other that particular kind of beauty which is the crown of our narcissism.

... At best, love is simply the slipping of a hand in another's, of knowing you are where you belong at last, and of exchanging through the eyes that all-consuming regard which ignores everybody else on earth.

Anonymous Elizabethan poem
contributed by Anne Zwack, Italy

> What thing is love
> For sure love is a thing
> It is a prick
> It is a sting
> It is a pretty, pretty thing.

Final verse of *Love's Offence* by Sir John Suckling
contributed by Elizabeth Cruse, London

> Then thus think I
>   Love is the fart
>   Of every heart:
> It pains a man when 'tis kept close,
> And others doth offend when 'tis let loose.

From *Annihilation* by Conrad Aiken
contributed by Michael Croft, Director, National Youth
Theatre of Great Britain

> Rock meeting rock can know love better
> Than eyes that stare or lips that touch.
> All that we know in love is bitter,
> And it is not much.

The Taste of Love

We are now into romance, 'the very burthen of the mystery,' and begin with a poem by Frances Cornford, great-niece of Wordsworth (who coined that phrase) grand-daughter of Charles Darwin (who wrote The Origin of Species), *wife of the professor of Ancient Philosophy at Cambridge, life-long friend of Rupert Brooke and key figure in the Bloomsbury Group.*

She had to live down two early epigrammatic fragments that made her notorious among literary sophisticates: To a Fat Lady Seen from a Train *('Why do you walk through the field in gloves/Missing so much and so much?') and, worse still in its mythogenic effect, the celebrated quatrain on Rupert Brooke ('A young Apollo, golden-haired/Stands dreaming on the edge of strife/Magnificently unprepared/For the long littleness of life') or short littleness as it was to be in Brooke's case.*

Two women sent Who has not seen: *Brenda Houghton (another philosopher by training, I can reveal from personal knowledge) who had read it in a newspaper as a schoolgirl and was able to reproduce it impeccably twenty-five years later; and Margaret Brock, who knew the name of the author, but seems to have read it in the same place, for she adds: 'Treasured for twenty-five years.'*

I cannot share their unreserved admiration, if only because the line 'Who has not seen their lover' grates on my conservatively syntactical mind. 'Who has not seen her lover' is, I suppose, sexist nowadays, but it is a better line, as indeed would be his lover. Still, the notion of the face in the crowd, the one dimly limned outline in the hurly-burly of the public place, is nicely caught.

A poem by Frances Cornford
contributed by Margaret D. Brock, Salisbury and Brenda
Houghton, London

> Who has not seen their lover
> > Walking at ease
> With usual feet that cover
> A pavement under trees;
> > Not singular, apart
> But featured, footed, dressed
> Approaching like the rest
> In the same dapple of the sunlight caught
> > And thought:
> Here comes my heart.

Next Neruda, a massive talent whose densely wrought images triumphantly leap the hurdles of language. I should much enjoy reading him in the Spanish, but it is a tribute to his power that his compact and polished clusters of ideas come through so well in English. The Italian poet Cesare Pavese pulls off a parallel success in his translucent In the Morning. *Another condensed miracle of solid poetic geometry is contained in the four lines of Pasternak's* Meeting. *Again, one regrets not having the Russian, but is totally seized by his elegant and glitteringly clean symbolism.*

So, inevitably, to Yevtushenko. How and why poets in Soviet Russia have become as celebrated as pop stars I don't profess to understand; the colossal sales and packed audiences must seem vast to the point of vulgarity in the eyes of our own cocooned makers. Yet again, though, Yevtushenko cuts through the language barrier to take our throats with the grip of his images. 'When she drops her overcoat on a chair/it will slide to the floor in a blue heap'; and our imaginations will do the rest.

The thrall of the dying fall, that throwaway line at the end of a poem which crystallises the whole of what has gone before, works its familiar magic in two short poems both sent by Patricia Groser: The Song of Annam *and the* Japanese Street Song. *But we don't need to look any further than our own islands for poetry of similar intensity: next we have a set of three –* The Lover's Shirt, *from the Welsh, as fresh and charming as if it were written yesterday, the four lines from the Old Irish spoken by the legendary Crainne, in which the notion of gladly giving up all the world can offer for one man's love recurs hauntingly yet again, and* The Bonnie Broukit Bairn *by Hugh M'Diarmid, said by its sender, Vi Hughes, to be one of the greatest love poems of the 20th century, and clearly magnificent by any standards; nor, I submit, in need of translation, though Vi Hughes generously provides one.*

From *I Ask For Silence* by Pablo Neruda, translated by Alastair Reid
contributed by Yvonne Gee, Ilford, Essex

> I only want five things,
> five chosen roots.
>
> One is an endless love.
>
> Two is to see the autumn.
> I cannot exist without leaves
> flying and falling to earth.
>
> The third is the solemn winter,
> the rain I loved, the caress
> of fire in the rough cold.
>
> My fourth is the summer,
> plump as a watermelon.

And fifthly, your eyes.
Matilde, my dear love,
I will not sleep without your eyes,
I will not exist but in your gaze.
I adjust the spring
for you to follow me with your eyes.

In the Morning You Always Come Back by Cesare Pavese,
translated by Iris Origo
contributed by Mrs Grenville Gore Langton, Easton,
Hampshire

The glimmer of dawn
breathes with your mouth
at the end of the empty streets.
Your eyes are grey lights,
sweet drops of dawn
on the dark hills.
Your passing and your breath
like the wind of dawn
overwhelm the houses.
The city is trembling,
the stones give forth their odour –
you are life, awakening.

Lost star in the light of dawn
twittering of the breeze,
warmth and breath –
the night is over.

You are the light and the morning.

From *Meeting* by Boris Pasternak, translated by Eugene M. Kayden
contributed by P. J. Robbins, Church Stretton, Salop

> It seems as if your image
> Drawn fine with pointed steel
> Is now in silver lines
> Cut deep upon my heart.

Waiting by Yevgeny Yevtushenko
contributed by Mrs S. Goodwin, Etchingham, East Sussex

My love will come
will fling open her arms and fold me in them,
will understand my fears, observe my changes.
In from the pouring dark, from the pitch night
without stopping to bang the taxi door
she'll run upstairs through the decaying porch
burning with love and love's happiness
she'll run dripping upstairs, she won't knock,
will take my head in her hands,
and when she drops her overcoat on a chair,
it will slide to the floor in a blue heap.

Stranger Things Have Happened (Song of Annam)
contributed by Patricia Groser, Abingdon, Oxfordshire

Do not believe that ink is always black,
    Or lime white, or lemon sour;
You cannot ring one bell from two pagodas,
You cannot have two governors for the city of Lang Son.

I found you binding an orange spray
Of flowers with white flowers;
I never noticed the flower gathering
Of other village ladies.

Would you like me to go and see your father and mother?

Drink Song (Japanese Street Song)
contributed by Patricia Groser, Abingdon, Oxfordshire

> The crows have wakened me
> By cawing at the moon.
> I pray that I shall not think of him;
> I pray so intently
> That he begins to fill my whole mind.
> This is getting on my nerves;
> I wonder if there is any of that wine left.

The Lover's Shirt (16th century Welsh poem)
contributed by Mrs Eurwen Mascall, Swansea

> As I was washing
> Under an arch of Cardigan Bridge,
> With a golden drubber in my hand
> And my love's shirt beneath it,
> A horseman came by,
> Wide-shouldered, quick, and proud.
> He asked me to sell
> The shirt of the one I love best,
> And I told him bluntly,
> Not for any money,
> Or the two hillsides
> covered with a flock of sheep,

> Or two fields full of yoked oxen,
> Or St David's stuffed to the rafters
> With trodden herbs.
> That's how I hang on to my loved one's shirt.

Old Irish Poem, translated by Gerald Murphy
contributed by Geraldine Pinch, Oxford

> There is one
> On whom I should glady gaze,
> For whom I would give the bright world,
> All of it, all of it, though it be an unequal bargain.

The Bonnie Broukit Bairn (Sangschawl) by Hugh M'Diarmid
contributed by Vi Hughes, Oxford

> Mars is braw in crammasy,
> Venus in a green silk goun,
> The auld moon shak's her gowden feathers,
> Their starry talk's a wheen o' blethers,
> Nane for thee a thochtie sparin',
> Earth, thou bonnie, broukit bairn!
> – But greet, an' in your tears ye'll drown
> The haill clanjamfrie!

We cannot call the next group of three English poets for MacNeice was of course an Irishman; nor can we properly call them all Thirties poets for the Laureate is still as I write very much with us and still at work; much past his best, no doubt, but with a substantial corpus of lovely work behind him, not least the enchanting In A Bath Tea Shop. *Did he see the lovers there, one*

cannot help asking, and the answer must surely be yes. No one pulls off better than Betjeman the sudden jerk of the rug from under our feet; the first couplet sugared as the cakes before the oblivious pair; the next vinegar-tart. And then, rather unusually for the Laureate when he's in this mood, a third couplet to restore us to the mellow snuggery of the opening lines.

Auden's Lullaby *('Lay your sleeping head, my love') is his most famous short poem; carefully wrought so that the sex of the loved one is ambiguous. Whether they are the four best lines in the lovely thing is anybody's guess, but Christopher Brightman who sent them clearly thought so, and we shall stand by his judgment. Amazingly, Auden was going to leave this out of his revised* Collected Shorter Poems *in 1965; his friend Chester Kallman persuaded him to put it back in.*

But, first, MacNeice's haunting Meeting Point. *Rosemary Bartlett, who sent it, commented that she knew she was cheating slightly because I'd already let slip my weakness for MacNeice. It was a shrewd move on her part and earned her a bottle of bubbly.*

Meeting Point by Louis MacNeice
contributed by Rosemary Bartlett, Birmingham

> Time was away and somewhere else,
> There were two glasses and two chairs
> And two people with the one pulse
> (Somebody stopped the moving stairs):
> Time was away and somewhere else.
>
> And they were neither up nor down;
> The stream's music did not stop
> Flowing through heather, limpid brown,
> Although they sat in a coffee shop
> And they were neither up nor down.

The bell was silent in the air
Holding its inverted poise—
Between the clang and clang a flower
A brazen calyx of no noise:
The bell was silent in the air.

The camels crossed the miles of sand
That stretched around the cups and plates;
The desert was their own, they planned
To portion out the stars and dates
The camels crossed the miles of sand.

Time was away and somewhere else.
The waiter did not come, the clock
Forgot them and the radio waltz
Came out like water from a rock:
Time was away and somewhere else.

Her fingers flicked away the ash
That bloomed again in tropic trees:
Not caring if the markets crash
When they had forests such as these,
Her fingers flicked away the ash.

God or whatever means the Good
Be praised that time can stop like this,
That what the heart has understood
Can verify in the body's peace
God or whatever means the Good.

Time was away and she was here
And life no longer what it was,
The bell was silent in the air
And all the moon aglow because
Time was away and she was here.

From *Lullaby* by W. H. Auden
contributed by Christopher Brightman, Sevenoaks, Kent

> Let the winds of dawn that blow
> Softly round your dreaming head
> Such a day of sweetness show
> Eye and knocking heart may bless,
> Find the mortal world enough.

In a Bath Tea-Shop by Sir John Betjeman
contributed by S. Williams, Clwyd

> 'Let us not speak, for the love we bear one another –
> Let us hold hands and look.'
> She, such a very ordinary little woman,
> He, such a thumping crook,
> But both of them little lower than the angels
> In the teashop's ingle-nook.

Now a cluster from antiquity, each conveying over the centuries the same shiver of recognition. Our anonymous 5th century Greek consigns her lover (or is it his?) to Lethe with a last poignant promise – and admonition. Philetas of Samos composed his touching elegy nearly a thousand years earlier; Brenda Davies, who sent it, said she was 'not yet quite fifty but heading that way'. The Song of Songs, *once attributed to Solomon himself, is now thought on linguistic grounds to be much later, perhaps around the time of Philetas, but whether we think of thirty or a mere twenty-five centuries, the clout of the poetry is equally stunning.*

Anonymous (5th century A.D.)
contributed by Barbara Rawson, Chard, Somerset

> This, noble Sabinus, is but a stone,
> a very small token to record a love
> as great as ours: I shall forever search
> for you. I ask only, if it be permissible
> down there among the departed – for
> my sake, do not drink from the waters
> of forgetfulness!

Philetas of Samos
contributed by Mrs B. M. Davies, Cheltenham

> Love,
> I offer you
> my sandals
> the glory of my hair
> my bronze mirror
> my girdle
> and what must remain
> unknown to men,
> for I am fifty
> and it is time
> to take stock.

From *Song of Songs* Ch. vii, verses 10-12
contributed by Mrs George Crawshaw, Bridport, Dorset

> I am my beloved's,
> And his desire is toward me.
> Come, my beloved, let us go forth into the field;

Let us lodge in the villages,
Let us get up early to the vineyards;
Let us see whether the vine hath budded,
   and its blossom be open,
And the pomengranates be in flower:
There will I give thee my love.

Under Milk Wood was described by Dylan Thomas as prose with blood pressure, and one sees what he means. This wonderful speech by Mog Edwards, the draper mad with love for Myfanwy Price at the sweet-shop, is about five minutes into the play, and was the first to get a real laugh from the audience when it was first performed in America.

Next, two oddities: Blue Sky, *claimed with some justice, I suspect, to be the shortest sonnet in the world; and the six lines from Swinburne's* The Oblation, *whose curiosity lies in the fact that they were written, not to a girl but to Italy, would you believe.*

Then two poems by living authors: The Snow, *a gentle piece already published here and in America but submitted now by the author himself, and the lyrical* Epithalamion *by Dannie Abse, doctor and poet, no doubt echoing Spenser's lovely hymn to marriage with the same title, and not, to my mind, overshadowed even in such company.*

From *Under Milk Wood* by Dylan Thomas
contributed by John David, Mere,

I am a draper mad with love. I love you more than all the flannelette and calico, candlewick, dimity, crash and merino, tussore, crettone, crepon, muslin, poplin, ticking and twill in the whole Cloth Hall of the world. I have come to take you away to my Emporium on the hill, where the change hums on wires. Throw away your little bedsocks and your Welsh wool knitted jacket, I will warm the sheets like an electric toaster, I will lie by your side like the Sunday roast.

Blue Sky (Anon)
contributed by Ian Edwards, London

I
Through
Blue
Sky
Fly
To
You.
Why?
Sweet
Love
Feet
Move
So
Slow

From The Oblation *(Songs Before Sunrise)* by A. C. Swinburne
contributed by Ronald Mason, Banstead, Surrey

I that have love and no more
Give you but love of you, sweet:
He that hath more, let him give;
He that hath wings, let him soar;
Mine is the heart at your feet
Here, that must love you to live.

The Snow by John Inglis Hall
contributed by the author, Balcombe, Sussex

> You are like snow.
> When you come to me
> Silence descends on the noisy earth,
> Wheel sounds are muffled,
> Walkers slink by with padded feet,
> The note of the neighbourhood's music
> Changes its key.
> As, inexorably and with sculptor's fingers,
> You fill up my wrinkles,
> In my bones I know
> That the touch of your body lingers
> Long after your fall is forgotten.
> Soaked in you,
> My corners and rough edges
> Take the curve of your breast and thigh.
> I need only remember the snow
> And how it lies smooth on the flesh
> For you to be for ever fresh
> In my mind's eye

Epithalamion by Dannie Abse
contributed by Joan and Gerry Anholt, London

> Singing, today I married my white girl
> beautiful in a barley field.
> Green on thy finger a grass blade curled,
> so with this ring I thee wed, I thee wed,
> and send our love to the loveless world
> of all the living and all the dead.

Now, no more than vulnerable human,
we, more than one, less than two,
are nearly ourselves in a barley field –
and only love is the rent that's due
though the bailiffs of time return anew
to all the living but not the dead.

Shipwrecked, the sun sinks down harbours
of a sky, unloads its liquid cargoes
of marigolds, and I and my white girl
lie still in the barley – who else wishes
to speak, what more can be said
by all the living against all the dead?

Come then all you wedding guests:
green ghosts of tress, gold of barley,
you blackbird priests in the field,
you wind that shakes the pansy head
fluttering on a stalk like a butterfly;
come the living and come the dead.

Listen flowers, birds, winds, worlds,
tell all today that I married
more than a white girl in the barley –
for today I took to my human bed
flower and bird and wind and world,
and all the living and all the dead.

Evelyn Waugh wrote Brideshead Revisited *during the first half of 1944 while recuperating from a minor injury incurred on military service. It was a bleak time – the period of soya beans and Basic English as Waugh put it – and in reaction the book was infused*

with what he called a kind of gluttony, not merely for food and wine, but also for the recent past, and for rhetorical and ornamental language.

Brideshead *was an immediate success, though Waugh later said that it lost him such esteem as he had once enjoyed among his contemporaries. It was Cecil Beaton's favourite book, and Nancy Mitford loved it but Cyril Connolly did imitations of Lord Marchmain's death scene. When the book was re-set in 1960, Waugh revised it fairly thoroughly, making small additions and large cuts. Even so, he did not excise what he called the grosser passages altogether; they were essential to the whole.*

He was probably right, though the impressionable young who fell for the book when it first came out revelled in the unashamed lushness. The passage chosen by John Gibbons for this anthology, where Charles and Julia consummate their love at the height of the Atlantic storm, was one of those which proved most vulnerable to critical attack. 'Now on the rough water, as I was made free of her narrow loins' got a particular hammering. In the revised passage that John Gibbons quotes, that is rewritten, though the words 'narrow loins' survive. A comparison between the two versions remains instructive, and an excellent proof of Quiller-Couch's laconic advice to the writer on style: Kill your darlings.

From *Brideshead Revisited* by Evelyn Waugh
contributed by John Gibbons, Leicester

In that minute, with her lips to my ear and her breath warm in the salt wind, Julia said, though I had not spoken, 'Yes, now,' and as the ship righted herself and for the moment ran into calmer waters, Julia led me below.

It was no time for the sweets of luxury; they would come, in their season, with the swallow and the lime flowers. Now on the rough water there was a formality to be observed, no more. It was as though a deed of conveyance to her narrow loins had been drawn and sealed. I was making my first entry as the freeholder of a property I would enjoy and develop at leisure.

'Is The Gold Hat included?' wrote Jill Parker. 'I'm not sure of its pedigree but think Scott Fitzgerald uses it on the flyleaf of The Great Gatsby *and signs it d'Invilliers.' He did indeed use it, but d'Invilliers is not a pseudonym for Fitzgerald, as is often believed. He was a real poet, though a curiously elusive one; I'm bound to say I've never read another line of his. It's almost as if his whole career was justified by those precisely right lines that introduce us to the thrall of Gatsby. 'I bet you know the verse,' Jill Parker went on, 'but never mind, I adore it.' That makes two of us.*

From the flyleaf of *The Great Gatsby* by Thomas Parke d'Invilliers
contributed by Jill Parker, London

> Then wear the gold hat, if that will move her;
> If you can bounce high, bounce for her too,
> Till she cry 'Lover, gold-hatted, high-bouncing lover,
>   I must have you!'

Light relief now from Edward Lear, artist and author, who got the Earl of Derby's children to laugh so much at his nonsense that he put it between hard covers to our benefit; from the immortal Groucho Marx; and from an anonymous country quatrain of limited applicability, one would have thought.

From *The Owl and the Pussycat* by Edward Lear
contributed by Jane V. Beaty, Berkhamsted, Herts.

> The owl looked up to the stars above,
>   And sang to a small guitar,
> 'O lovely Pussy, O Pussy, my love,
>   What a beautiful Pussy you are,
>   You are
>   You are!
>   What a beautiful Pussy you are!'
>
> Pussy said to the Owl, 'You elegant fowl,
>   How charmingly sweet you sing!
> Oh! let us be married; too long we have tarried:
>   But what shall we do for a ring?'

From the final scene of *A Day at the Races* – Groucho Marx:

'Emily, will you marry me – I will never look at another horse.'

Valentine rhyme (Anon)

> We were courting by the bridge
> My lips were all a-quiver
> But then your wooden leg dropped off
> And floated down the river.

Finally in this section four wildly different instances of love declared: Peter Wimsey puts it across in French (a good example of the upper-class love scene now, as I suggested in the introduction, toppling over into farce); the moment of truth for doctor and nun in The Story of San Michele *(where in a bourgeois context much the same stricture might be said to apply); the extraordinary scene from Dante's* Inferno – *to my mind the most erotic in this book; and finally, in Gabriel Oak's declaration to Bathsheba Everdene, surely the most romantic proposal in fiction – though Bathsheba resists it till the last few lines of the book.*

From *Busman's Honeymoon* by Dorothy L. Sayers
contributed by Sue Chambers, Beverley, Yorkshire

He had turned and said, suddenly and huskily:
'Tu m'enivres!'
Language and voice together had been like a lightning-flash, showing up past and future in a single crack of fire that hurt your eyes and was followed by a darkness like thick, black velvet....

From *The Story of San Michele* by Axel Munthe
contributed by John Gibbons, Leicester

I looked at the rigid, cruel face of the old Abbess which even death had not been able to soften. It was almost a relief to me that her eyes were closed for ever ... I looked at the young nun by my side.
'I cannot stay here any longer,' I said, 'I have not slept since I came here, my head is swimming ... I am afraid of myself, I am afraid of you, I am afraid of ...' I had not time

to finish the word, she had not time to draw back, my arms had closed round her, I felt the tumultuous beating of her heart against my heart.

'Pieta!' she murmured.

Suddenly she pointed towards the bed and sprang out of the room with a cry of terror. The eyes of the old Abbess were looking straight at me, wide-open, terrible, menacing.

From Canto V of Dante's *Inferno*
contributed by D. J. Cheke, Basingstoke

> One day, for pastime, we read of Lancelot, how
>   love constrained him; we were alone, and
>   without all suspicion.
>
> Several times that reading urged our eyes to
>   meet, and changed the colour of our faces;
>   but one moment alone it was that overcame us.
>
> When we read how the fond smile was kissed
>   by such a lover, he who shall never be
>   divided from me
>
> Kissed my mouth all trembling: the book, and
>   he who wrote it, was a Galeotto; that day
>   we read in it no farther.

From *Far From The Madding Crowd* by Thomas Hardy
(Gabriel Oak proposes to Bathsheba Everdene)
contributed by Mary Schoenfeld Smith, Malmesbury

'And at home by the fire, whenever you look up, there shall I be – and whenever I look up, there will you be'.

The Thrust of Love

Now we move on to the province of passion and the fleshly expression of love. If we start with a slightly improper quatrain of Anon's, it is because it is a delightful one, and sent by more than one reader. The faux-naif opening couplet is suddenly countered by the delicious interior rhyme of line three and the ripe, round blasphemy of line four seals in the whole concoction.

The notion of love-in-violence is explored literally by Robert Browning, and metaphorically by Pierce Ferriter. No truthful work on love could be complete without a little discreet bottom-pinching somewhere, and we have a charming example in the French of Roland Dubillard.

When I first read The Zoo of You I had a hunch it was written by a Californian. I was nearly right; it was written by Arthur Freeman as a Havard undergraduate in the Fifties and he's been trying to suppress it ever since. Well, I persist in liking it. Maybe it wobbles a bit in the middle, but as Arthur points out, he was all of nineteen when he wrote it (and he has written some highly accomplished stuff since, by the way). There was another problem: 'My wife (on whom my erotic attentions are now fixed) does indeed have copper hair, but these puling lines were written some fifteen years before we met, and she suspects they aren't about her.'

We sent some peace-bringing golden fizz to Mr and Mrs Freeman (he now works as rare book consultant to the London firm Bernard Quaritch) and became friends over it. Now another hazard looms: someone wants to incorporate it in an American musical. Arthur Freeman gloomily predicts that it will end up on Broadway.

51

Contributed by Charles Hennessey, Bridgnorth, Shropshire

> Flo, Flo, I love you so
> I love you in your nightie;
> When the moonlight flits across your tits –
> Jesus Christ Almighty!

From *Porphyria's Lover* by Robert Browning
contributed by David Jenkins, Bridgend

> Be sure I looked up at her eyes
>   Proud, very proud; at last I knew
> Porphyria worshipped me; surprise
>   Made my heart swell, and still it grew
> While I debated what to do.
> That moment she was mine, mine, fair,
>   Perfectly pure and good: I found
> A thing to do, and all her hair
>   In one long yellow string I wound
> Three times her little throat around,
> And strangled her.

By Pierce Ferriter, translated by the late Lord Longford
and quoted in Brendan Behan's *Island*
contributed by Ian Ward, Ware

I charge you, lady, young and fair, straightaway to lay your
    arms aside.
Lay by your armour – would you dare to spread the
    slaughter far and wide?
O lady, lay your armour by, conceal your curling hair also,
For never was a man could fly the coils that o'er your
    bosom flow.

And if you answer, lady fair, that north or south you ne'er
    took life
Your very eyes, your glance, your air can murder without
    axe or knife.
And O if you but bare your knee – if you your soft hand's
    palm advance,
You'll slaughter many a company – what more is done
    with shield or lance?

O hide your bosom limey-white, your naked side conceal
    from me
And show them not in all men's sight, your breasts more
    bright than flowering tree.
And if in you there's shame or fear for all the murders you
    have done,
Let those bright eyes no more appear – those shining teeth
    be seen of none.

Lady, we tremble far and near, be with these conquests
    satisfied,
Unless they perish, lady dear, O lay those arms of yours
    aside.

From *Naives Hirondelles* (The Swallows) by Roland Dubillard, translated by Barbara Wright
contributed by J. P. Turnbull, Norwich

Bertrand: At least I hope you remember, the evening you
    arrived, do you remember I pinched your bottom?

Germaine: Oh Bertrand! I know you didn't do it on
    purpose!

The Zoo of You by Arthur Freeman

> Thy leopard legs and python thighs,
> Thy perchèd breasts and darting eyes,
>
> Thy growling belly in its lair,
> Thy crafty copperhead of hair,
>
> Thy silky calves and furry groins,
> Thy maney, rippling lion-loins,
>
> Thy hind-behind, all these pursue
> In beastly order (and I too)
>
> Thy Pussy's primitive purlieu.
> Unlock! Unlock! Let's feed thy zoo.

That first entry of Nabokov's Lolita *is still a show-stopper: the page itself seems to curl at the edge in the heat. What a writer! It's difficult to remember now all the fuss that greeted* Lolita's *debut: the protesters seem to have melted. Verity Bargate in* No Mama No *makes a virtue too out of straightforward sexual candour. The things that happen to one in the middle of Pricerite.*

Ricky Amy sent what she calls 'this brassy little gem' from the lascivious pen of the scribe who wrote the Chester Beatty Papyrus I in Egypt around 1100 BC, and Liz Sowal sent the Sanskrit poem Black Marigolds: *'I suspect it was given to me by my then boyfriend. Ah youth! Regrettably I am not, and indeed never was, even twenty years ago, quite so beautiful as the lady in the poem. Still, it was gratifying at the time to think there must have been any resemblance, however slight. I hope you think it as beautiful as I do. Very sensual, but still love, I think.'*

Diana Leigh sent the quotation from American novelist James Branch Cabell in block capitals from the Barbican; it lingers in the mind.

From *Lolita* by Vladimir Nabokov
contributed by Paul Oswald, Braintree, Essex

Lolita, light of my fire, fire of my loins. My sin, my soul. Lo-lee-ta: the tip of my tongue taking a trip of three steps down the palate to tap, at three, on the teeth. Lo. Lee. Ta.

She was Lo, plain Lo, in the morning, standing four feet ten in one sock. She was Lola in slacks. She was Dolly at school. She was Dolores on the dotted line. But in my arms she was always Lolita.

It was the same child – the same frail, honey-hued shoulders, the same silky supple bare back, the same chestnut head of hair. A polka-dotted handkerchief tied around her chest hid from my aging ape eyes, but not from the gaze of young memory, the juvenile breasts I had fondled one immortal day. And, as if I were the fairy-tale nurse of some little princess (lost, kidnapped, discovered in gypsy rags through which her nakedness smiled at the king and his hounds), I recognised the tiny dark-brown mole on her side. With awe and delight (the king crying for joy, the trumpets blaring, the nurse drunk) I saw again her lovely indrawn abdomen where my southbound mouth had briefly paused; and those puerile hips on which I had kissed the crenellated imprint left by the band of her shorts – that last mad immortal day behind the 'Roches Roses'. The twenty-five years I had lived since then, tapered to a palpitating point, and vanished.

From *No Mama No* by Verity Bargate
contributed by Paul Oswald, Braintree, Essex

The mindless muzak suddenly stopped just being a background hum and I heard the Righteous Brothers' song 'You've lost that loving feeling', not very loud, a bit crackly, but unmistakeable.

I thought my heart would stop beating or that I might faint so intense was the pain I felt, but of course nothing at all happened; I was still standing there holding a packet of fish fingers, but ah! seven years ago it was caviar or nothing and it was love and it wasn't David and there was passion and music and flowers and there was somebody else's husband in a basement flat in Knightsbridge, and before that the only thing to seduce me into lying down and taking my clothes off had been the sun. I was so inexperienced that the first time we made love I didn't even notice that he only had one ball. Actually it was the third or fourth time, when I was able to open my eyes without blushing, and he told me he had had it shot off in the Korean war. I thought that was incredibly romantic and was also impressed because he was still in the RNVR; it seemed very patriotic and Rupert Brooke-ish, for Queen, Country and testicle. Strangely I discovered the reality only about a year ago when I met someone who was at university with him at the time of the accident.

Still, a bad pain to have in the middle of Pricerite.

By the scribe who wrote the Chester Beatty Papyrus 1 in Egypt around 1100 B.C.
contributed by Ricki Amy, London

> Why need you hold converse with your heart?
> (To embrace her is all my desire)
> As Amun lives! I come to you,
> My loin cloth on my shoulder.

Black Marigolds, translated from the Sanskrit
by E. Powys Mathers
contributed by Liz Souval, Bradford

Even now
Death sends me the flickering of powdery lids
Over wild eyes and the pity of her slim body
All broken up with the weariness of joy;
The little red flowers of her breasts to be my comfort
Moving above scarves, and for my sorrow
Wet crimson lips that once I marked as mine.

Even now
They chatter her weakness through the two bazaars
Who was so strong to love me. And small men
That buy and sell for silver being slaves
Crinkle the fat about their eyes; and yet
No Prince of the Cities of the Seas has taken her
Heading to his grim bed. Little lovely one
You clung to me as a garment clings; my girl.

Even now
I love long black eyes that caress like silk,
Ever and ever sad and laughing eyes
Whose lids make such sweet shadow when they close
It seems another beautiful look of hers.
I love a fresh mouth, ah, a scented mouth,
And curving hair, subtle as a smoke,
And light fingers, and laughter of green gems.

Even now
I remember that you made answer very softly
We being one soul, your hand on my hair,
The burning memory rounding your near lips.
I have seen the priestesses of Rati make love at moon fall
And then in a carpeted hall with a bright gold lamp,
Lie down carelessly anywhere to sleep.

Even now
If I see in my soul the citron-breasted fair one
Still gold-tinted, her face like our night stars
Drawing unto her; her body beaten about with flame
Wounded by the flaring spear of love,
My first of all by reason of her fresh years,
Then is my heart buried alive in snow.

Even now
If my girl with lotus eyes came to me again
Weary with the dear weight of young love
Again I would give her to these starved twins of arms
And from her mouth drink down the heavy wine,
As a reeling pirate bee in fluttered east
Steals up the honey from the nenuphar.

Even now
If I saw her lying all wide eyes
And with collyrium the indent of her cheek
Lengthened to the bright ear and her pale side
So suffering the fever of my distance
Then would my love for her be ropes of flowers, and night
A black-haired lover on the breasts of day.

Even now
My eyes that hurry to see no more are painting, painting
Faces of my lost girl. O golden rings
That tap against cheeks of small magnolia leaves
O whitest so soft parchment where
My poor divorced lips have written excellent
Stanzas of kisses, and will write no more.

By James Branch Cabell
contributed by Diana Leigh, London

A man possesses nothing certainly save a brief loan of his own body: and yet the body.... is capable of much curious pleasure.

A whole clutch of testimony to the body's rapture: the music of Yeats and the chatter of Stevie Smith; elegance from John Updike and comedy from Adrian Mitchell; a lofty come-hither from Conrad Aiken (much more cheerful than when we last heard from him); a sophisticated Valentine from New York; a coarse but telling tribute to beauty from The Arabian Nights. *'Thank you for the lovely weekend' was a late-night dedication on local commercial radio at Plymouth Sound. And the couplet about the saddle of a bike was written jointly by Betjeman, Auden, and MacNeice. It is said to be the shortest erotic poem; it is certainly one of the funniest.*

A last Confession by W. B. Yeats

> What lively lad most pleasured me
> Of all that with me lay?
> I answer that I gave my soul
> And loved in misery,
> But had great pleasure with a lad
>   That I loved bodily.

Flinging from his arms I laughed
To think his passion such
He fancied that I gave a soul
Did but our bodies touch,
And laughed upon his breast to think
   Beast gave beast as much.

I gave what other women gave
That stepped out of their clothes,
But when this soul, its body off,
Naked to naked goes,
He it has found shall find therein
   What none other knows,

And give his own and take his own
And rule in his own right;
And though it loved in misery
Close and cling so tight,
There's not a bird of day that dare
   Extinguish that delight.

Conviction (4) by Stevie Smith
contributed by Brenda Lawrence, London

I like to get off with people,
I like to lie in their arms,
I like to be held and tightly kissed,
Safe from all alarms.

I like to laugh and be happy
With a beautiful, beautiful kiss,
I tell you, in all the world,
There is no bliss like this.

Pale Bliss by John Updike
contributed by Gilly Bisson, Guernsey

> Splitting a bottle of white wine
> With a naked woman
> In the middle of the day.

Celia, Celia by Adrian Mitchell
contributed by Thekla H. W. Howell

> When I am sad and weary,
> When I think all hope has gone,
> When I walk along High Holborn
> I think of you with nothing on.

From *Preludes for Memnon LII* by Conrad Aiken
contributed by Michael Croft, Director, National Youth
Theatre of Great Britain

> The hour is early, and the speech is late.
> Come, we are gods – let us discourse as gods;
> And weigh the grain of sand with Socrates;
> Before we fall to kissing, and to bed.

Valentine (Anon)
contributed by John Inglis Hall, Balcombe, Sussex

> My fancy and face in New York!
> A Valentine's dry pillow talk
> For a kissable broad,
> Untumbled, adored,
> Deep sea twixt your flower and my stalk.

From Burton's translation of *The Arabian Nights*
contributed by Karl Sabbagh, Richmond, Surrey

.... all who looked on her bepissed their bag trousers, for
the excess of her beauty and loveliness.

Anon
contributed by Gordon West, Tavistock, Devon

> Thank you for a lovely weekend.
> They tell me it rained.

The shortest erotic poem – written jointly by Betjeman,
Auden, and MacNeice
contributed by Mrs Keith Darby, Wolverhampton

> I often think that I would like
> To be the saddle of a bike

*After our whole-hearted celebration of carnal pleasure, let us have a
brief hiatus before plunging on again to consider three very different
poems about idealised or unobtainable love: the delicate line of Guido
Cavalcanti, first friend to Dante; the aching regret in the verse of
Arnaut Daniel, called by Petrarch the first master of love and here
translated by Ezra Pound; and the gossamer touch of the Hindu poet
Rabindranath Tagore. This last was sent by Barbara Taylor, who
has lived many years in India, and believes, with some justice I*

think, that we have made far too little effort to understand the Oriental mind. I'm ashamed to say I have passed Tagore's old house on Hampstead Heath hundreds of times, noting the blue plaque recording his years there, but until now never coming to grips with his poetry.

By Guido Cavalcanti
contributed and translated by Ken Lake, London

> Who is she, whom all men
>   gaze on
> And who makes the air
>   tremulous with light?
> And leads one with her love,
> So that no man can speak
>   but each one sighs.

By Arnaut Daniel, translated from the French
by Ezra Pound
contributed by Ken Lake, London

> Only I know what over-anguish falls
> Upon the love-worn heart through over-love.
> Because of my desire so firm and whole
> Toward her I loved on sight and since always,
> Which turneth not aside nor wavereth.
> So, far from her, I speech mad speech,
> Who near her, for o'er much to speak, am dumb.

From *The Fugitive Cycle* by Rabindranath Tagore
contributed by Barbara Taylor, Warminster

My songs are like bees; they follow through the air some fragrant trace – some memory – of you, to hum around your shyness, eager for its hidden store.

When the freshness of dawn droops in the sun, when in the noon the air hangs low with heaviness and the forest is silent, my songs return home, their languid wings dusted with gold.

The Worst of Love

The literature of lost love is vast, but also consoling: it teaches us we are not alone when we lose love. Jane Austen puts the case for the greater longevity of woman's love with economical power in Persuasion: *Anne Elliot, the speaker, is often said to have been modelled on Jane herself; it could be. The words spoken by Gloria Grahame to Humphrey Bogart in a still much underrated film could hardly be written now, but seemed right in the 1940s. The quote from* The Times Valentine *column, as reader Hinte in West Germany suggests, has a special appeal for music lovers and is ingenious even by the contortionate standards of that annual festival. Six short lines are all Sappho needs to convey the ache of a lonely bed; Gabriel Chevallier fills in the minutiae with remarkable empathy for a man.*

Thomas Hardy wrote some of his greatest poems after the death of his wife, and the one we give here has, as Elizabeth Whittome observes, one of the most beautiful final stanzas ever written. Yevtushenko eloquently catches the fear of loss to come; and lastly in this section a haunting eight lines from Shirley Jones who believes they are by Shakespeare. Not so; nor are they Donne or Yeats; and I remain baffled yet strangely beguiled by them.

From *Persuasion* by Jane Austen
contributed by Mrs B. P. Hubbard, Bath

'All the privilege I claim for my own sex (it is not a very
enviable one: you need not covet it), is that of loving
longest, when existence or when hope is gone!'

   She [Anne Elliot] could not immediately have uttered
another sentence; her heart was too full.

Gloria Grahame to Humphrey Bogart in Nicholas Ray's *In
a Lonely Place*
contributed by Peter Smith, London

'I was born when you kissed me. I died when you left me. I
lived a few days while you loved me.'

From *The Times,* 14 February 1981
contributed by Dr Paul Hinte, West Germany

> Magic Flute, my dream Byrd,
> you Ravel passions Haydn in me
> I haven't felt Fauré long Weill:
> come Bach to Britten and we'll
> Pleyel those duets in eternal
> Bliss. Bleib treu XXX dein piggy
> on the fiddle.

Sappho, 600 B.C., translated by J. M. Edmonds
contributed by the Reverend John Bickley, Brandon,
Suffolk

> The Moon is gone
> And the Pleiads set,
>   Midnight is nigh;
> Time passes on,
> And passes, yet
>   Alone I lie.

From *Clochmerle-Babylon* by Gabriel Chevallier
contributed by Mrs S. Potts, Scarborough

In her bed the widow feels isolated, as when she was a girl,
but minus the sweet presentiments of the future. And
when, after tossing and turning in a discomfort of body
and soul, she falls asleep at last, it is in the knowledge that
when she wakes it will not be to hear that rough but
beneficent voice which gave her courage, that her naked
shoulder will not feel the roughness of a bristly chin, that
she will not have to disentangle herself from a body as hard
and massive as a pier to which, in her sleep, she has
moored herself while her mind was gently rocked on the
waves of her dreams.

The Voice by Thomas Hardy
contributed by Mrs Elizabeth Whittome, Horsmonden,
Kent

Woman much missed, how you call to me, call to me,
Saying that now you are not as you were
When you had changed from the one who was all to me,
But as at first, when our day was fair.

Can it be you that I hear? Let me view you, then,
Standing as when I drew near to the town
Where you would wait for me: yes, as I knew you then,
Even to the original air-blue gown!

Or is it only the breeze, in its listlessness
Travelling across the wet mead to me here,
You being ever dissolved to wan wistlessness,
Heard no more again far or near?

    Thus I; faltering forward,
    Leaves around me falling,
Wind oozing thin through the thorn from norward,
    And the woman calling.

Colours by Yevgeny Yevtushenko, translated by Herbert Marshall
contributed by Julie Harrison, Hertford

    When your face
    appeared over my crumpled life
    at first I understood
    only the poverty of what I have.
    Then its particular light
    on woods, on rivers, on the sea,
    became my beginning in the coloured world
    in which I had not yet had my beginning.
    I am so frightened, I am so frightened,
    of the unexpected sunrise finishing,
    of revelations
    and tears and the excitement finishing.
    I don't fight it, my love is this fear,

I nourish it who can nourish nothing,
love's slipshod watchman.
Fear hems me in.
I am conscious that these minutes are short
and that the colours in my eyes will vanish
when your face sets.

contributed by Shirley Jones, Northampton

I'll bark against the Dog Star,
I'll crow away the morning,
I'll chase the moon 'til it be noon
And I'll make her leave her horning.

But I'll find Merry Mad Maudlin
And seek whate'er betides her
And I will love, beneath, above
The dirty earth that hides her.

*When Sir Ronald Storrs, diplomatist and scholar, died in 1955, he
left behind several hundred verse translations of Horace's* Ode to
Pyrrha *(Book I, Ode 5) which he had been collecting for a book. It
was published in 1959, and included translations by Gladstone,
Milton, Edward Marsh, L. S. Amery, John Simon, Maurice Baring,
Duff Cooper, D. B. Wyndham Lewis ('Beachcomber') and a young
infantry captain called Simon Raven. At that time 451 translations
were known to exist, not only into English, but also into Czech,
Maltese, Russian, Turkish, Welsh, and so on. Such is the
extraordinary fascination of Horace's ode to a fickle, golden-haired
girl. With the decline of the classics, the tally of new attempts to*

*unravel its densely worked magic will doubtless climb more slowly;
but it was cheering indeed to see one reader, Betty Mutton, have a
shot at the opening three lines unprompted. I have tried to persuade
her to do the remaining eleven, but she says no, her Latin is no longer
up to it. Never mind, here is her free-swinging version of the
opening, and may publication encourage her to finish it off for our
next edition.*

Horace Book I Ode V – to Pyrrha
contributed and translated by Betty Mutton, Maidstone

'Who's the dishy young man, Pyrrha, with the gorgeous
after-shave chatting you up on the patio under the roses?'

*'The poor wretch who wrote these lines was a most exceptional
suicide,' comments Aldous Huxley of* No wish to die. *'How
moving it is! And, in its way how beautiful! The rhythm of the
sentences is perfect. And those repetitions at the close are managed
with what, were the writer a deliberate artist, would be a most
exquisite felicity.'*

*Well said – and it might be added that the unconscious elegance
of the close is accentuated by the comic coarseness of what has gone
just before:* 'This b---- at Palmer's Green has sneaked my wife'. *Bert
Harrison, who sent it, said it had stayed in his memory these last
forty-five years.*

Cited by Aldous Huxley in *Texts and Pretexts* – a letter
written by a man just before he killed himself
contributed by Bert Harrison, Kenilworth

No wish to die. One of the best of sports, which they all
knew. Not in the wrong, the boys will tell you. This b---- at
Palmer's Green has sneaked my wife, one of the best in the
world; my wife, the first love in the world.

Anon's Western wind, when wilt thou blow *finds its way into
most anthologies, and rightly; it was sent by a number of readers.
Adrian Henri gets a modern come-uppance and puts it over in just
two witty lines. Cherry Gilliam wrote that she wouldn't bother
placing bets on how many extracts from* Le Grand Meaulnes *were
winging their way towards me; we chose hers. No book of this kind
would be complete without something of Scott Fitzgerald's and this
extract from* The Last Tycoon *serves the bill well: note the switch
to a trivial point at the end of the paragraph to cleanse the palate.
The letter from the superintendent of an iron foundry to the wife of
an inspector of customs is a masterpiece of unconscious humour and
we must be grateful to the lady who received it for having the wit to
preserve it for us. The sonnet by Duff Cooper is frankly a touch
square, but has a certain curiosity value for idle minds. For his
marriage to Lady Diana Manners – still happily with us as I
write – is one of the great love stories of the century. Whose love was
it he couldn't win? And to end this section, that menacing and
mysterious poem by Stevie Smith, another persistently popular poet
with readers.*

Annonymous 16th century poem
contributed by Thomas Higgins, Manchester

> Western wind, when wilt thou blow
> The small rain down can rain?
> Christ, if my love were in my arms
> And I in my bed again!

Song for a Beautiful Girl Petrol-Pump Attendant on the
Motorway by Adrian Henri
contributed by Dr T. O. Craig, Mottram-in-Longdendale,
Cheshire

> I wanted your soft verges
> but you gave me the hard shoulder.

From *Le Grand Meaulnes* by Alain-Fournier
contributed by Cherry Gilliam, Doddington, Kent

As Mademoiselle de Galais was leaving the house,
Meaulnes went towards her, and taking up the conversation where she had dropped it, said:
  'The name I gave you was a more beautiful one.'
  'Really? And what was it?' Her face remained grave.
  But thinking he might have blundered again, he kept it
to himself.
  'Mine is Augustin Meaulnes. I'm a student.'
  And for a few moments they talked in a leisurely way,
with enjoyment like friends. Then there was a change in
the girl's manner. Less distant now, and less grave, she
seemed more uneasy. It was as if she dreaded what
Meaulnes might be going to say and recoiled in advance.
She was quivering at his side, like a swallow which had
come to rest for an instant but was already trembling with
the wish to resume its flight.

And when he began to speak of his hopes she replied gently:

'But what's the use? ... What's the use?'

And yet when at last he summoned up courage to ask permission to return one day to his wonderful domain, she said quite naturally:

'I shall be expecting you.'

They came in sight of the landing stage. She stood still a moment, then said, pensively:

'We're both children. We've been foolish. We must not go back in the same boat. Goodbye – don't follow me.'

Disconcerted, Meaulnes stood and watched her move away. A little later when he too had reached the shore, he saw her turn, before losing herself in the distant throng, to look back at him. For the first time her eyes rested on him in a steady regard. Was it meant as a final farewell? Was she forbidding him to accompany her? Or was there perhaps something more she would have liked to say?...

From *The Last Tycoon* by Scott Fitzgerald
contributed by Paul Oswald, Braintree, Essex

Now they were different people as they started back. Four times they had driven along the shore road today, each time a different pair. Curiosity, sadness, and desire were behind them now; this was a true returning – to themselves and all their past and future and the encroaching presence of tomorrow. He asked her to sit close in the car, and she did, but they did not seem close, because for that you have to seem to be growing closer. Nothing stands still. It was on his tongue to ask her to come to the house he rented and sleep there tonight – but he felt it would make him sound lonely. As the car climbed the hill to her house, Kathleen looked for something behind the seat cushion.

From the superintendent of an iron foundry to the wife of an inspector of customs in the Southern States, 1877

Dear Madam,

Although I am fully aware of the robust condition of your husband's health, and of your tender affection for him and your little ones, I am impelled by a sense of the propriety of providing in time for the casualties and fortuities of the future, to ask your permission, in case of your (at present unexpected) widowhood, to renew the addresses which were broken off by your marriage to your present estimable consort.

Yours respectfully,

John Pickett

By Duff Cooper
contributed by Dr Raymond Greene, London

Of many nights I shall remember one –
A night of music, wine and gaiety,
When hopes were high for once, and hearts were free
For once, and when for once the world was fun.
Even before the east foretold the sun
We found the fierce refreshment of the sea,
Where like a ghost your body swam to me,
Cold as the dawn, and whiter than the swan.
'Cold, cold, my girl!' You know Othello's cry
To his lost love. Love's warm but beauty's cold –
As cold and clear as star-lit winter sky.
Your love I could not win, but I can hold
The vision of your beauty manifold,
Deep in my heart until the day I die.

The Warden by Stevie Smith

> They played in the beautiful garden
> Those children of high degree
> But she sighed as she swam with the Warden
> In the depths of the Zuyder Zee.
>
> O why did you take me away
> From the children I loved so well?
> I had other plans in my heart, dear
> For the child of my latest spell.
>
> The Warden had decked her with seaweed,
> And shells of an ancient design,
> But she sighs as she presses his fingers,
> My heart can never be thine.
>
> He sits in the golden chair,
> With the child he would call his own,
> But the beautiful child has expired,
> He nurses a sea-green stone.

One striking feature of the mailbag was the popularity of Dorothy Parker. War Song *is described by Eric Caulton as one of her very rare sentimental pieces. I dunno. Bitter-sweet I should have said.*

Look Homeward Angel *was Thomas Wolfe's first novel, published when he was twenty-nine. He was a giant of a man (six feet six) with a giant talent and a torrent of words in him of which this extract is a fair sample.* Young Lad of the Braided Hair *has something of the same torrential feel about it, vast though the gap in time and place between the two.*

To end the section, a charming envoi from the French: no race pays that sort of compliment better.

War Song by Dorothy Parker
contributed by B. E. Caulton, Shepton Mallet, Somerset

> Soldier in a curious land,
> All across a swaying sea,
> Take her smile and lift her hand –
> Have no guilt of me.
>
> Soldier, when were soldiers true?
> If she's kind and sweet and gay,
> Use the wish I send to you,
> Lie not lone till day.
>
> Only, for the nights that were,
> Soldier, and the dawns that came,
> When in sleep you turn to her,
> Call her by my name.

From *Look Homeward Angel* by Thomas Wolfe
contributed by Maurice Nelson, Croydon

Come up into the hill, O my young love. Return! O lost, and by the wind grieved, ghost, come back again, as first I knew you in the timeless valley, where we shall feel ourselves anew, bedded on magic in the month of June. There was a place where all the sun went glistering in your

hair, and from the hill we could have put a finger on a star. Where is the day that melted into one rich noise? Where the music of your flesh, the rhyme of your teeth, the dainty languor of your legs, your small firm arms, your slender fingers, to be bitten like an apple, and the little cherry teats of your white breasts? And where are all the tiny wires of finespun maidenhair? Quick are the mouths of earth, and quick the teeth that fed upon this loveliness. You who were made for music, will hear music no more: in your dark house the winds are silent. Ghost, ghost, come back from that marriage that we did not foresee, return not into life, but into magic, where we have never died, into the enchanted wood, where we still lie, strewn on the grass. Come up into the hills, O my young love: return, O lost and by the wind grieved, ghost, come back again.

Young Lad of the Braided Hair (Irish Trad.)
contributed by John Baldwin, Bristol

Young lad of the braided hair with whom I was a while together, you went this way last night and did not come to see me. I thought it would do you no harm if you came to seek me, and that a little kiss of yours would give me comfort if I were in the midst of a fever. If I had wealth and money in my pocket I should have a short cut made to the door of my love's house, hoping to God I should hear the sweet sound of his shoe and for many a day I have not slept but in hopes for the taste of your kiss. And I thought my sweetheart, that you were the moon and the sun, and I thought after that, that you were the snow on the mountain, and I thought after that, that you were lightning from God, or that you were the Pole Star going before and behind me. You promised me silk and satin, hoods and shoes with high heels, and you promised after that, that you would follow me swimming. I am not like that, but like a hawthorn in the 'gap' every evening and every morning watching my mother's house.

From *La Nouvelle Heloise* by Jean-Jacques Rousseau contributed and translated by Mrs Doraine Potts, Headington

Julie de l'Espinasse to Monsieur de Guibert in 1774

My dear, I am in torment, I love you and await you.

Dated: every moment of my life

The Twist of Love

The literature of disillusioned love must equal the literature of lost love. From Samuel Johnson's chilly view of marriage to Dorothy Parker's mordant Love Song, *from Hilaire Belloc's sad quatrain to Tennyson's world-weary couplet, from the plastic metaphors of Bjorn Nilsen to the tepid similes of Ezra Pound the message is the same: is that all there is to it?*

From *Rasselas* by Samuel Johnson
contributed by David Jenkins, Bridgend

Such is the common process of marriage. A youth and maiden, meeting by chance or brought together by artifice, exchange glances, reciprocate civilities, go home, and dream of one another. Having little to divert attention, or diversify thought, they find themselves uneasy when they are apart, and therefore conclude that they shall be happy together. They marry, and discover what nothing but voluntary blindness before had concealed: they wear out life in altercations, and charge nature with cruelty.

Love Song by Dorothy Parker
contributed by Mrs Lyn Jackson, Birchington, Kent

> My own dear love, he is strong and bold
> And he cares not what comes after.
> His words ring sweet as a chime of gold,
> And his eyes are lit with laughter.
> He is jubilant as a flag unfurled –
> Oh, a girl, she'd not forget him.
> My own dear love, he is all my world –
> And I wish I'd never met him.
>
> My love, he's mad, and my love, he's fleet.
> And a wild young wood-thing bore him!
> The ways are fair to his roaming feet.
> And the skies are sunlit for him.
> As sharply sweet to my heart he seems
> As the fragrance of acacia.
> My own dear love, he is all my dreams –
> And I wish he were in Asia.
>
> My love runs by like a day in June,
> And he makes no friends of sorrows.
> He'll tread his galloping rigadoon
> In the pathway of the morrows.
> He'll live his days where the sunbeams start,
> Nor could storm or wind uproot him.
> My own dear love, he is all my heart –
> And I wish somebody'd shoot him.

The False Heart by Hilaire Belloc
contributed by Mrs Patricia Elton, Clevedon, Avon

> I said to heart, 'How goes it?' Heart replied:
> 'Right as a Ribstone Pippin!' But it lied.

By Tennyson
contributed by Mrs Patricia Elton, Clevedon, Avon

He shall hold thee, when passion shall have spent its novel
    force,
A little closer than his dog, a little dearer than his horse.

By Bjorn Nilsen
contributed and translated by Penny English and Eric
Barber, Norway

> Take my plastic flowers
> and my duplicated love-letters
> with adjectives chosen by admen.
> Take my marshmallow heart
> and say yes.
> Then we can go
> and have a cassette tape join us
> in everlasting wedlock to the building society.
> Put on your best clothes
> and your freshest smile
> let's pretend to be people.

From *The Bath Tub* by Ezra Pound
contributed by Ken Lake, London

As a bath tub lined with white porcelain,
When the hot water gives out or goes tepid,
So is the slow cooking of our chivalrous passion,
O my much praised but-not-altogether-satisfactory lady.

Not many memories get away to a better racing start than Harriet Wilson's. Though written in 1825, there is something totally modern about some of her phraseology, notably when she describes Lord Craven's notions of entertainment as a dead bore. It was the manuscript of this book which provoked the Duke of Wellington's celebrated 'Publish and be damned!' As Adam Rowntree remarks, happily she did, and he doesn't believe she was.

From Harriet Wilson's Memoirs (1825)
contributed by Adam Rowntree, London

I shall not say why and how I became, at the age of fifteen, the mistress of the Earl of Craven. Whether it was love, or the severity of my father, the depravity of my own heart, or the winning arts of the noble Lord, which induced me to leave my paternal roof and place myself under his protection, does not now much signify: or if it does, I am not in the humour to gratify curiosity in this matter.

I resided on the Marine Parade at Brighton; and I remember that Lord Craven used to draw cocoa trees, and his fellows, on the best vellum paper for my amusement. Here stood the enemy he would say; and here my love, are my fellows, etc. It was in fact a dead bore. All this at past eleven o'clock at night, could have no peculiar interest for a child like myself, so lately in the habit of retiring early to rest....

See the mothers in the park *is by an unknown author: Cassie Diamond heard a young American comedian recite it some years ago and it has lived with her. The kinky link between love and bondage may strike some people as optimistic, but I think not. Our Romans Catullus and Horace (again) undoubtedly knew the scourge of love. The Chinese lady in* The Western Window *sounds disenchanted; but then so does the Chinese gentleman in* The Bad Road *('they shut her heart in a box of iron'); nor does our Burmese poet sound much less bitter. Madame de Staël puts the whole bloody female dilemma in a neat nutshell; Dorothy Parker comes on for an encore and delivers a closing coup-de-grace.*

Contributed by Cassie Diamond, Woodford Green, Essex

> See the mothers in the park,
> Ugly creatures chiefly.
> Someone must have loved them once,
> In the dark, and briefly.

Contributed by Mrs Bobbie Prime, Nottingham

> Love is bondage
> Willingly accepted by the free.

Catullus
contributed by David Williams, London

> I hate and I love. Why do I do it? perhaps you ask;
> I do not know, but I feel it, and it is torture.

Horace, translated by Sir Theodore Martin
contributed by the Reverend John Bickley, Brandon,
Suffolk

> I myself, wooed by one who was truly a jewel,
>   In thralldom was held, which I cheerfully bore.
> By that common chit Myrtile, though she was cruel
>   As waves that indent the Calabrian shore.

The Western Window (from the Chinese of Wang Ch'ang
Ling, 8th century)
contributed by Patricia Groser, Abingdon, Oxfordshire

> At the head of a thousand roaring warriors,
> With the sound of gongs,
> My husband has departed
> Following glory.
>
> At first I was overjoyed
> To have a young girl's liberty.
>
> Now I look at the yellowing willow-leaves;
> They were green the day he left.
>
> I wonder if he also was glad?

The Bad Road (from the Chinese)
contributed by Patricia Groser, Abingdon, Oxfordshire

> I have seen a pathway shaded by green great trees,
> A road bordered by thickets light with flowers.
>
> My eyes have entered in under the green shadow,
> And made a cool journey far along the road.
>
> But I shall not take the road,
> Because it does not lead to her house.
>
> When she was born
> They shut her little feet in iron boxes,
> So that my belovèd never walks the roads.
>
> When she was born
> They shut her heart in a box of iron,
> So that my belovèd shall never love me.

Canker in the Heart (19th century Burmese)
contributed by Patricia Groser, Abingdon, Oxfordshire

> I made a bitter song
> When I was a boy,
> About a girl
> With hot earth-coloured hair,
> Who lived with me
> And left me.
>
> I made a sour song
> On her marriage-day,
> That ever his kisses
> Would be ghosts of mine,
> And ever the measure
> Of his halting love
> Flow to my music.

It was a silly song,
Dear wife with cool black hair,
And yet when I recall
(At night with you asleep)
That once you gave yourself
Before we met,
I do not quite well know
What song to make.

By Madame de Staël
contributed by Mrs O. Cannon, Bideford, Devon

Love is the history of a woman's life; it is an episode in
  man's.

From *The Choice* by Dorothy Parker
contributed by W. A. B. Macdonald, Nelson, Lancashire

He'd have given me laces rare,
    Dresses that glimmered with frosty sheen,
Shining ribbons to wrap my hair,
    Horses to draw me, fine as a queen.
You – you'd only to whistle low,
    Gaily I followed wherever you led.
I took you, and I let him go –
    Somebody ought to examine my head!

The Best of Love

*Despite all the heartaches and the thousand natural shocks that love
is heir to, men and women persist, in and out of marriage, in finding
lasting happiness together. We begin this section with a quite
splendid hors d'oeuvre from a Victorian marriage manual, and
follow it with testaments to two Edwardian marriages of unusual
duration and serenity. Even Winston and Clemmie had their ups and
downs, as we now know from Mary Soames's magisterial biography
of her mother. Winston had one rule I've always found rather
puzzling: never, as he would put it, to let the sun go down on his
wrath. One would have thought it much better after a marital tiff to
sleep it off and not let the sun come* up *on your wrath, but* quot
homines tot sententiae. *We also have a remarkable account of the
relationship between Harold and Vita from the book by their son
Nigel Nicolson; here reciprocal infidelities and homosexual predilec-
tions were balanced by mutual affection and shared interests; by love
indeed, of a rare kind, as Vita testifies.*

Courtship and Matrimony (from a Victorian manual of
etiquette)
contributed by Mrs Joyce Holt, Fleet, Hampshire

The young bride, divested of her bridal attire, and quietly
costumed for her journey, now bids farewell to her
bridesmaids and lady friends.

A few tears spring to her gentle eyes as she takes a last look at the home she is now leaving. The servants venture to crowd around her with their humble but heartfelt congratulations; finally she falls weeping on her mother's bosom.

A short cough is heard, as of someone summoning up enough resolution to hide an emotion. It is her father. He dares not trust his voice; but holds out his hand, gives her an affectionate kiss and then leads her, half turning back, down the stairs and through the hall to the door, where he delivers her as a precious charge to her husband, who hands her quickly into the carriage, springs in after her, waves his hand to the party who appear crowding at the windows, half smiles at the throng about the door, then, amidst a shower of old slippers – missiles of good luck, sent flying after the happy pair – gives the word and they are off, and started on the long-hoped-for voyage.

From a letter written by Vita Sackville-West to Harold Nicolson in 1929
contributed by Trevor Seed, Southport

..... You are dearer to me than anybody ever has been or ever could be. If you died suddenly, I should kill myself as soon as I had made provision for the boys. I really mean this. I could not live if I lost you. I do not think one could conceive of a love more exclusive, more tender, or more pure than I have for you. I think it is immortal, a thing which happens seldom.

Darling, there are not many people who would write such a letter after sixteen years of marriage, yet who would be saying therein only one-fiftieth of what they were feeling as they wrote it. I sometimes try to tell you the truth, and then I find that I have no words at my command which could possibly convey it to you.

Letter from Winston to Clementine Churchill (quoted in
Mary Soames' biography, *Clementine*)
contributed by Mrs S. Verinder, Worthing

You ought to trust me for I do not love and will never love
any woman in the world but you, and my chief desire is to
link myself to you week by week by bonds which shall ever
become more intimate and profound.
Beloved I kiss your memory – your sweetness and beauty
have cast a glory upon my life.
You will find me always
Your loving and devoted husband
W.

*Now a whole garland of poetry celebrating the delights and rewards
of constancy in love: MacNeice again, tenderly concise; Pound
putting his finger on a particular and precious moment in the cycle of
long days together; our unknown medieval German saying it with
beguiling simplicity; Wang Chia working the dying fall; one
medieval French poet declaring his total commitment and another
French poet giving us a beguiling object lesson from the natural
world. Ausonius defying age to weary his love; Robert Graves
exploring the memory of love between sleep and waking; John Gower
weaving a medieval counterpoint on the theme of* odi et amo; *Amy
Lowell accepting gladly the bland savour of mellowed passion; and
D. H. Lawrence wielding his talent like a paint brush to conjure a
sensual female figure from the life class in his mind.*

From *Leaving Barra* by Louis MacNeice
contributed by A. A. C. Page, Epsom, Surrey

> And you who to me among women
> Stand for so much that I wish for,
> I thank you, my dear, for the example
> Of living like a fugue and moving.
>
> For few are able to keep moving,
> They drag and flag in the traffic;
> While you are alive beyond question
> Like the dazzle on the sea, my darling.

From *The Garret* by Ezra Pound
contributed by Ken Lake, London

> Dawn enters with little feet
> like a gilded Pavlova,
> And I am near my desire.
> Nor has life in it aught better
> Than this hour of clear coolness,
> the hour of waking together.

Medieval German Poem
contributed by Louise Farroll, Oakridge Lynch

> You are mine, I am yours:
> that is how it must be.
> You are locked
> in my heart;
> the key is lost:
> you must stay there forever.

Ancient Theme by Wang Chia
contributed by Sue Ball, Brighton

You are on duty at the Hsiao Pass, I am here in Wu;
The west wind blows on me, and I am anxious for you.
For one line of this letter there are a thousand lines of tears.
When winter reaches you, will your warm clothes have
    reached you?

15th/16th century French poem, quoted in *Checkmate* by
Dorothy Dunnett
contributed by Mrs Sheila Bryant, Chislehurst, Kent

> Long as I live, my heart will never vary
> For no one else, however fair or good
> Brave, resolute or rich, of gentle blood,
> My choice is made, and I will have no other.

The Lay of the Honeysuckle (French, Anonymous)

> They two were like the honeysuckle, and
> the hazel which it clings to ...
> together they can long endure, but
> if anyone should try to separate them
> the hazel dies at once and the honeysuckle
> too. My sweet love, so it is with us:
> you cannot live without me, nor I
> without you.

By Ausonius (4th century scholar and poet)
contributed by Mrs H. Taylor, Almondbury, Huddersfield

> Love, let us live as we have lived, nor lose
> The little names that were the first night's grace,
> And never come the day that sees us old,
> I still your lad and you my little lass.
> Let me be older than old Nestor's years
> And you the Sibyl, if we heed it not.
> What should we know, we two, of ripe old age?
> We'll have its richness, and the years forgot.

She Tells Her Love While Half Asleep by Robert Graves

> She tells her love while half asleep,
> In the dark hours,
> With half-words whispered low:
> As Earth stirs in her winter sleep
> And puts out grass and flowers
> Despite the snow,
> Despite the falling snow.

By John Gower
contributed by Jane Wolff, Eastbourne

> O thou my sorwe and my gladnesse,
> O thou my hele and my sikenesse,
> O thou my wanhope and my trust,
> O thou my disease and all my lust,
> O thou my wele, O thou my wo,
> O thou my frende, O thou my fo,
> O thou my love, O thou my hate,
> For the mote I be dede algate.
> Thilk ende may I nought afterte,
> And yet with all min hole herte,
> While that there lasteth me any breth,
> I woll the love unto my deth.

A Decade by Amy Lowell
contributed by Joy Bell, Bristol

When you came, you were like red wine and honey,
And the taste of you burnt my mouth with its sweetness.
Now you are like morning bread,
Smooth and pleasant.
I hardly taste you at all for I know your savour,
But I am completely nourished.

Gloire de Dijon by D. H. Lawrence
contributed by Mr. F. Browne, Harrogate

When she rises in the morning
I linger to watch her;
She spreads the bath-cloth underneath the window
And the sunbeams catch her
Glistening white on the shoulders,
While down her sides the mellow
Golden shadow glows as
She stoops to the sponge, and her swung breasts
Sway like full-blown yellow
Gloire de Dijon roses.

She drips herself with water, and her shoulders
Glisten as silver, they crumple up
Like wet and falling roses, and I listen
For the sluicing of their rain-dishevelled petals.
In the window full of sunlight
Concentrates her golden shadow
Fold on fold, until it glows as
Mellow as the glory roses.

Four remarkable letters: and we are privileged to publish the one from William Walker to his wife for the first time. It was sent by his grandson, also a William Walker, and has been in the family since 1857, when the elder William sent it to his wife on the birth of their first born child. The grandson has his grandparents' marriage certificate dated 27 October 1856 on which the husband is described as a warehouseman aged twenty-three, his wife a servant aged nineteen. 'I think you will agree,' says the present Mr Walker, 'that from a man of little education it breathes love and tenderness and simplicity.' It does indeed; qualities that might well have been ironed out by formal education.

The poignancy of Thomas Wedderburn's letter is of course infinitely multiplied by the postscript; while William Taylor was clearly a natural poet. If I hesitate over the last of the quartet, it's only because I wonder if we're condescending to it; but I think not.

A letter written in 1867 by a warehouseman aged twenty-three to his wife, a servant aged nineteen, on the birth of their first born
contributed by William Walker, Bradford

My dearest wife,

I cannot tell you the feelings that agitated my bosom when I received the welcome news of your safe delivery I scarcely knew what to do when I saw that I (sic) we had a son born to us. I saw that God had been better to us than all our fears but to tell the truth I was most happy to hear

that you were safe. Do dearest be carefull for all danger is
not over yet. Do not get up to soon but I can trust to
mother for that dear Chigg I hope that our infant son may
be the means of binding (if Possible) our hearts more
closely together so that whatever trials we may be called to
by the providence of God that our sincere love for one
another and for our offspring may always abound Give my
dear boy a kiss from is delighted father and accept the
same yourself. I hope that I shall soon be able to clasp you
both to my heart. The letter that your kind sister sent does
not mention any particulars now I shall wait till you get up
and as soon as you are able to write and let me know if he
as a bit in the low lip and what color is eyes are You may
think that I am qeer writed but you do not know what it
is to be a father. Dear Chigg you must not make yourself
uneasy about me.

I conclude hoping soon to hear from you

I am your most affectionate husband

William Walker

Give my love to mother and all enquiring friends and give
dear Herbert a kiss And be sure that you take plenty of
gruel

Letter written in 1746 on the eve of the Battle of Culloden
contributed by Mrs D. Morland, London

My dear,

I am now in my quarters, it is about eleven at night … I
cannot go to bed until I tell you that I never think myself
entire but when I am with you. I would be very happy if I
could now lye down in your arms … You do give me, and
can continue to give me, all the pleasure that a wife I love

can give; you afford me all the happiness that a virtuous companion can produce in a mind already full of you. It is in your power to make me more miserable than I can tell you, it is beyond expression, it is more than possibly you can imagine. I am satisfied of the truth and strength of our affection and hope it shall end only with life itself. In the strictest truth of my heart, I assure you, I am wholly yours..... God bless you and our dear boy, I am your affectionate and faithfull husband, Thos Wedderburn.

He was killed in the battle on the following day.

Letter by an unknown lover in humble life, picked up on the beach at Sidmouth in 1887 and quoted in Mrs A. M. W. Stirling's biography of William De Morgan.

My Dearest Marey, – i be verry well an appey to inform you that i be very well at present and i hope you be the same dear Marey – i be verry sorry to hear how as you don't like your quarters as i chant be able to look on your dear face so offen as i have done dearest Marey, pure and holy meek and loly loveley Rose of Sharon. Dear Marey, dear Marey i hant got now know particler noose to tell ye at present but my sister that marryd have got sich a nice lettel babey, and i wish how as that our littel affare was settled and we had got such a nice lettel dear two.

Dearest Marey i shall not be appy till then Dearest Marey pure and holy meek and loly lovely Rose of Sharon. Sometimes i do begin to despare as i am affraid our not will never be tide but my Master have prommist i how as that when i get ye he will putt ye in the Darey yard to feed the Piggs and ge ye atin pens a week Dearest Marey pure and holey meek and loly lovely Rose of Sharon. i be comming over tomorrow to by the Ring and you must come to the stayshun to mete me and bring a pese of string with you the size of your finggar and be shure you don't make A miss take dear Marey.

Father is A going to ge us a beddsted and Granny A 5 lb note to by such as washin stand fier irons mouse trap and Sope, and wee must wayte till wee can by carpetting and glass crackery ware and chiny. Dearest Marey pure and holy meek and loly lovely Rose of Sharon, i be very appy to say our old Sow As got 7 young uns laste nite and Father is a going to ge us A roosester for our Weding Brakefast Dearest Marey pure and holey meek and loly lovely Rose of Sharon. So no more at present from your fewture and loving husband,

William Taylor

Quoted from a newspaper report in *Love*
by Walter de la Mare
contributed by Mrs M. E. Cook, Dundee
and Ronald Mason, Banstead

Dear Alf,
   I seen you last night in my dream. O my dear I cried at waking up. What a silly girl you been and got. The pain is bad this morning but I laugh at the sollum clocks of the sisters and the sawbones. I can see they think I am booked but they don't know what has befalen between you and me. How could I die and leave my Dear. I spill my medecin this morning thinking of my Dear. Hoping this finds you well no more now from yours truly, Liz

The Last of Love

In my end is my beginning. Be with me darling, early and late: the fight against loneliness which is at the core of love's universal appeal to human kind is eloquently realised in Love Poem *by the American poet John Frederick Nims, often called the American MacNeice; hence perhaps his appearance here.*

In this anthology and in all others, two giant figures recur continuously. Both grow in stature as the years carry them away from us, as we can stand back and try to gauge their towering stature. The Song of Wandering Aengus *has a transcending beauty that puts it, in my view,* hors concours; *and only Hardy from that generation seems fit to take his place beside him among the immortals;* An Undying Story *is a miracle made from bare and simple words into thoughts at the edge of language.*

Let us climb down from that high place and play at being small again with A. A. Milne and Pooh and Christopher Robin. Not everybody's cup of tea, this. Our old friend Dorothy Parker gave Milne's Pooh play Give Me Yesterday *the old heave-ho in a 1931* New Yorker *('My dearest dread is the word 'yesterday' in the name of a play; for I know that sometime during the evening I am going to be transported, albeit kicking and screaming, back to the scenes and costumes of a tenderer time'). Somerset Maugham's anecdote is guilty, I fear, of inverted sentimentality if not downright condescension again, but clearly it has moved at least one reader, and may move more.*

I should be somewhat more in favour of Francoise Delisle, to whom Havelock Ellis wrote so touchingly, if she had not, by her own testimony, seen him several times in the week after his death. I prefer the lovely finality of the Book of Ruth.

from *Love Poem* by John Frederick Nims
contributed by George Gouldsbrough, Burnley

Be with me, darling, early and late. Smash glasses –
I will study wry music for your sake.
For should your hands drop white and empty
All the toys of the world would break.

The Song of Wandering Aengus by W. B. Yeats
contributed by Mrs Elizabeth Whittome, Horsmonden, Kent

I went out to the hazel wood
Because a fire was in my head,
And cut and peeled a hazel wand,
And hooked a berry to a thread;
And when white moths were on the wing,
And moth-like stars were flickering out,
I dropped the berry in a stream
And caught a little silver trout.

When I had laid it on the floor
I went to blow the fire aflame,
But something rustled on the floor,
And someone called me by my name.
It had become a glimmering girl
With apple blossom in her hair
Who called me by my name and ran
And faded through the brightening air.

Though I am old with wandering
Through hollow lands and hilly lands,
I will find out where she has gone,
And kiss her lips and take her hands;
And walk among long dappled grass,
And pluck till time and times are done
The silver apples of the moon,
The golden apples of the sun.

An Undying Story by Thomas Hardy
contributed by the Reverend C. F. Warren, Newport,
Gwent

> Only a man harrowing clods
> In a slow and silent walk
> With an old horse that stumbles and nods
> Half asleep as they stalk,
>
> Only thin smoke without flame
> From the heaps of couch grass;
> Yet this will go onward the same
> Though Dynasties pass.
>
> Yonder a maid and her wight
> Come whispering by:
> War's annals will cloud into night
> Ere their story die.

From *The House At Pooh Corner* by A. A. Milne
contributed by Mrs Carole Malone, Colchester, Essex

'Pooh, promise you won't forget about me, ever. Not even when I'm a hundred.'

Pooh thought for a little. 'How old shall I be then?'

'Ninety-nine.'

Pooh nodded. 'I promise,' he said.

Still with his eyes on the world Christopher Robin put out a hand and felt for Pooh's paw.

'Pooh,' said Christopher Robin earnestly, 'if I – if I'm not quite – ' he stopped and tried again – 'Pooh, whatever happens, you will understand, won't you?'

From *A Writer's Notebook* by W. Somerset Maughan
contributed by Pamela Paul, Ongar, Essex

She was a tallish woman, with reddish, untidy scanty hair, and when she opened her mouth you saw that two of her front teeth were missing. One of her ears was partly torn off by her husband, and there was a scar on her forehead which was the result of a cut when once he had thrown her out of a window. He was a big, strong, brutal fellow who had been badly wounded in the war, and Mrs Bailey forgave him his violence because he was often in great pain. They had four children and they all went in terror of him. But Mrs Bailey had a strong sense of humour, the real Cockney humour, and when she wasn't in fear of her life was full of fun. She loved a good laugh. At last Bailey died. I went to see her after his death, and she said to me – 'He wasn't a bad man really. D'you know what he said to me? They was almost his last words. "I've given you hell haven't I? You'll be glad to be rid of me." "No I won't, Ned," I said to him, "you know I've always loved you." He gave me a funny look, and d'you know what he said? "You old cow," he said. That shows he loved me really doesn't it? – calling me an old cow like that, I mean.'

Letter from Havelock Ellis to Francoise Delisle (from *Friendship's Odyssey* by Francoise Delisle)
contributed by Hilda Macdonald, Leigh-on-Sea, Essex

My Darling Naiad,
  This is the last letter you will ever receive from me, so I want to say over again – though I have said it so often before – with what deep love in my heart I shall leave you. I want to say again, too, that you must not feel I am dead. Those whom we love go on living in our hearts as long as we live …

When I first met you I thought my life was over. In one sense perhaps it was. But the happiest years of my life have been with you. I had never dreamed such happiness possible for me. These years still seem a miracle. And even the troubles in our life have still left love untouched. That love has never been disturbed for one moment …

My ever lasting love to my darling Naiad.

From the Book of Ruth
contributed by Gil Thomas, Bath

Intreat me not to leave thee, or to return from following
    after thee:
for whither thou goest, I will go; and where thou lodgest, I
    will lodge:
thy people shall be my people, and thy God my God:
Where thou diest, will I die, and there will I be buried.

It would be a deprivation to finish without something from the pen of C. S. Lewis, here at his most cogent and consoling; no wonder he brought his pupil Kenneth Tynan up to, but not quite through, the gates of belief.

Tibullus still moves us, twenty-two hundred years on, with four lapidary lines. What more would a Roman say? And since we cannot and must not end on a downbeat, let us give the last word to the unknown author of Pervigilium Veneris. *Just nine words in the Latin say it all, and four of those say it twice: whether you've loved before or no, love tomorrow; love tomorrow.*

From *A Grief Observed* by C. S. Lewis
contributed by Rosemary Pettit, London

And then one or other dies. And we think of this as love cut
short; like a dance stopped in mid career or a flower with
its head unluckily snapped off – something truncated and
therefore, lacking its due shape. I wonder. If, as I can't help
suspecting, the dead also feel the pains of separation (and
this may be one of their purgatorial sufferings), then for
both lovers, and for all pairs of lovers without exception,
bereavement is a universal and integral part of our
experience of love. It follows marriage as normally as
marriage follows courtship or as autumn follows summer.
It is not a truncation of the process but one of its phases;
not the interruption of the dance, but the next figure. We
are 'taken out of ourselves' by the loved one while she is
here. Then comes the tragic figure of the dance in which
we must learn to be still taken out of ourselves though the
bodily presence is withdrawn, to love the very Her, and not
fall back to loving our past, or our memory, or our sorrow,
or our relief from sorrow, or our own love.

By Tibullus (1st century B.C.)
contributed by Mrs Eve Cooper, London

> Let me behold thee
> when my last hour is come,
> Thee let me hold with
> my dying hand.

From *Pervigilium Veneris*
contributed by Ken Lake, London

> Let whoever never loved,
>   love tomorrow;
> Let whoever has loved,
>   love tomorrow.

Acknowledgements

I should like to thank Roger Houghton, editorial director of Elm Tree Books, whose happy idea it was to make this anthology, and Connie Austen Smith, my editor there, who guided me so skilfully through all the pitfalls of permission and copyright. I am most grateful to Frank Giles, editor of the *Sunday Times*, for giving the book his blessing, though equally I must make it clear that the responsibility for it is mine alone. Finally I must thank each and every reader who sent in nominations, whether I've used them or not. Surely no columnist could wish for a more agreeable, civilised and good-humoured audience; may they have as much pleasure from reading this book as I had in compiling it.

Grateful thanks are due to the following publishers and copyright holders for permission to reprint the extracts which appear in this book: The Bodley Head, Scott Fitzgerald and Charles Scribner's Sons for *The Last Tycoon* by Scott Fitzgerald; Arthur Freeman for *A Zoo of You* (© 1964); Robert Graves for *She Tells Her Love While Half Asleep* from *Collected Poems*; William Sloane Associates Inc., New York, for *Love Poem* from *The Iron Pastoral* by John Frederick Nims; the estate of Pablo Neruda, Alastair Reid (translator) and Jonathan Cape Ltd for *Pido Silencio* from *Extravagaria* by Pablo Neruda; Eugene M. Kayden (translator) and the Kent State University Press for *Meeting* from *Poems* by Boris Pasternak; McLelland Stewart Ltd, Toronto, and Methuen Children's Books for *The House at Pooh Corner* by A. A. Milne; Professor François Lafitte for *Friendship's Odyssey* by Françoise Delisle; John Inglis Hall for *The Snow*; Edmund A. Rennolds Jr and Margaret Freeman Cabell for the lines of James Branch Cabell; James MacGibbon (executor) for *The Warden* and *Conviction* from *The Collected Poems of Stevie Smith*; Adrian Henri and Jonathan Cape Ltd for *Song for a Beautiful Girl Petrol-Pump Attendant on the Motorway*; Dannie Abse for *Epithalamion* from *Collected Poems* (© 1977); Faber & Faber Ltd for *Lullaby* from *Collected Poems* by W. H. Auden, *Leaving Barra* and *Meeting Point* from *The Collected Poems of Louis MacNeice*, *The Garret* and *The Bath Tub* from *Collected Shorter Poems* by Ezra Pound and *A Grief Observed* by C. S. Lewis; John Murray Ltd for *In a Bath Teashop* by John Betjeman; Houghton Mifflin Company for *A Decade* by

Amy Lowell (© 1955); the Estate of Dylan Thomas for *Under Milk Wood* by Dylan Thomas; Dorothy L. Sayers for *Busman's Honeymoon;* Iris Murdoch and Chatto & Windus Ltd for *The Black Prince;* Robert Kotewall and Norman L. Smith (translators) and Penguin Books Ltd for *Ancient Theme* by Wang Chia from *The Penguin Book of Chinese Verse;* Pan Books Ltd for *Celia, Celia* by Adrian Mitchell from *Making Love: The Picador Book of Erotic Verse* (ed. Alan Bold); Laurence Pollinger Ltd and the Estate of the late Mrs Freda Lawrence Ravagli for *Gloire de Dijon* from *The Complete Poems of D. H. Lawrence;* Martin Secker and Warburg Ltd for *Clochemerle-Babylon* by Gabriel Chevallier (trans. E. Hyams); the Estate of Somerset Maugham; M. B. Yeats, Anne Yeats and Macmillan London Ltd for *The Song of Wandering Aengus* and *A Last Confession* from *Collected Poems of W. B. Yeats;* A. D. Peters & Co. Ltd for *Brideshead Revisited* by Evelyn Waugh; Collins Publishers for *We Speak No Treason* by Rosemary Hawley Jarman; Harrap Ltd for *Le Grand Meaulnes* by Alain-Fournier (ed. Gibson); George Allen & Unwin for *Autobiography 1872-1914* by Bertrand Russell; Lord Norwich for the poem by Duff Cooper; John Calder Ltd for *Naives Hirondelles (The Swallows)* by Roland Dubillard (trans. Barbara Wright); Victor Gollancz Ltd for *Colours* from *Love Poems* by Yevgeny Yevtushenko; Cassell Ltd and Times Newspapers Ltd for *Clementine* by Mary Soames; Duckworth Ltd for *The False Heart* from *Complete Verse of Hilaire Belloc* and *Soldier in a Foreign Land, Love Song* and *The Choice* from *The Collected Dorothy Parker;* Lord Longford for the late Lord Longford's translation of Pierce Ferriter; the Trustees of the Tagore Estate and Macmillan, London and Basingstoke for *The Fugitive Cycle* by Rabindranath Tagore; Weidenfeld & Nicolson Ltd for *Lolita* by Vladimir Nabokov; Axel Munthe and John Murray Ltd for *The Story of San Michele;* Andre Deutsch Ltd for *I Can't Stay Long* by Laurie Lee and *Pale Bliss* by John Updike; Oxford University Press, New York for *Annihilation* and *Preludes for Memnon LII* by Conrad Aiken.

Every effort has been made to trace the copyright holders of the extracts in this book. Should there be any omissions in this respect, we apologise and shall be pleased to make the appropriate acknowledgement in future editions.

INDEX OF FIRST LINES
(of passages quoted; not always of entire piece)